REFLECTIONS ON THE CREED

Hugh Lavery

REFLECTIONS
ON THE CREED

St Paul Publications

St Paul Publications
Middlegreen, Slough SL3 6BT, England

Copyright © St Paul Publications 1982
First published October 1982
Printed by the Society of St Paul, Slough
ISBN 085439 213 0

St Paul Publications is an activity of the priests
and brothers of the Society of St Paul who
promote the Christian message through the mass media.

Contents

I BELIEVE IN GOD

"I believe in God" is not an opinion. It is a decision. It decides everything important, and puts firm ground beneath your feet. It determines your stand in face of the landscape of your life; it gives point and purpose to the labour of living. Faith is glass. Through it you look out on this world and see the sunlight, the stars and the vast acres of infinity. Above all, it relays your vision of people, of your family and your friends. And it decides how you see yourself.

All men and women live and move by a creed. All have some fragmentary faith. In some it is strong as steel, in many blown like a leaf. But it is faith, and faith alone, that imparts drive and direction; faith which sparks ignition. Not a great brain, not muscle or beauty; these are ornaments. Faith is foundation. Men of talent, women of charm often achieve little and assign the cause to accident or malice. Yet this is alibi. Failure is not the child of misfortune; nor fulfilment the fruit of circumstance. Faith is the first agent of increase; unfaith of sterility. The option is ours.

History is a good teacher and contemporary history a good class-room. Pessimists speak of a loss of confidence. For a nation, like a person, can lose faith in itself, have no pride in its past, no belief in its future. The media talk of decline. The old are cynical and the young violent; and all blame the system. Gentle people call for reform; the angry for revolution. But all are troubled by a loss of confidence. This is well diagnosed. For confidence is faith in secular dress. When confidence wanes, all look for the man or woman of faith. A collective wisdom is aware that he or she alone can save them. For when the storm breaks all systems seem fragile, all theories false. We seek the person.

"Seek and you shall find", says Jesus. The juice of Christianity is distilled in this imperative. Few can accept this crisp command. Many subscribe to the dismal gospel of Macbeth. Hearing of his wife's death from a heart heavy with guilt he spoke a classic credo. "Life", he said, "is a tale told by an idiot, signifying nothing." If nothing signifies, if creation is mere accident, this planet just chemistry, people fickle and love an illusion, then life is useless expense and a waste of energy. Strange philosophies have grown on this mush of meaninglessness. "As flies to wanton boys we are to the gods; they kill us for their sport." This was the cry to Lear in his dementia; but not his alone. To live without meaning is the worst madness and no one is immune to this insanity.

And yet. Yet there is an instinct, a desire, almost a passion to believe. To believe in this world as good and touched with glory; to see life as precious, the gift that cannot be costed. The universe itself, so vast, so intricate, the variety of flowers, the fertility of fields, the appeal of sanctity, the innocence of the child, all conspire to move us to celebrate the wonder of being alive. Old songs, sublime poems, fine symphonies — how can we disclaim the presence of powers and dominations more real and more engaging than the hardware of the world? Wonder is the first gift and anoints the eyes of the innocent. To cease to wonder is to begin to die, for the eyes are listless, and the ears do not hear the hum of the true and eternal things which sustain that world which is too much with us. The need for bread is so urgent, the pursuit of money so compelling that living becomes breathless and the world is seen as a supermarket with alluring and well-laden shelves. Already we are dying, already failing to see, already unable to celebrate the wonder of this world.

Illusion and disillusion

"I believe in God" is a decision; here I take a stand. It is a declaration of dependence; of all men and of all things, on Someone above, beyond and within this empire. Nor is such a decision easily made. Though conscious of dependence, people resent it as they resent colonialism; it seems to degrade and demean them. They prefer to see this world as an autonomous entity, powered by its own batteries, a self-governing conglomerate. This does not remotely square with the facts; we are not our own makers. Yet it does minister to our variety for we want to be our own master. In the high Victorian age, men grew heady with the prospect of total command of the universe. Science would probe every nook and cranny of creation, root out every secret. Mystery would evaporate like vapour. God would be declared redundant; and the supreme being for man would be man. His sceptre would not be the sword. It would be the machine.

This intoxication held until the cataclysm of 1914. In Autumn fields, ripe for harvest, the machine became the machine-gun. Young men fell in disciplined rows to witness to its power and to reveal its malevolence. Stone crosses on village greens record the names of those who believed their valour would inaugurate the millennium for their children, and that the demon war would be finally exorcised. And yet their wounds were not waste, nor their deaths total disaster. When the guns spoke no more and poppies blew in the fields again, what followed was disillusion. And disillusion, though painful, is a teacher of unpalatable truths. The best medicine is often an astrigent. It is possible to pass our days screened by illusion. Only the wise accept disillusion as revelation. Of the truth. One man may regret his lost illusions and sicken with moroseness. Another will see it as release, life's first liberation. The truth has made him free and he sees the world through clearer glass no longer misted by illusion.

The question "Why?"

"I believe in God" sees the world mortgaged to God and not as man's domain. Man did not make it; nor can he understand it. We can climb its mountains, extract its minerals, explore its oceans, defile its beauty. What we cannot do is explain it. How did it begin? When will it end? How does the animal adapt and survive when its rain-forests are felled, and its plants no longer grow? Evolution is just one of the many mysteries that tease our intelligence and compel us to ask if there is not some power, infinitely more acute than any human wisdom, that is the matrix of this fine fecundity. For the universe does not carry its own explanation. We can only wonder at the great galaxies so far from our own. Science probes with its satellites and relays pictures of dead and gaseous planets. But the deep questions remain deep. And unanswered.

Yet the deepest question does not concern the universe. The question that most troubles us is, simply, me. Why am I here? What am I to do? The spider knows it must spin a web. The bee knows it must gather honey. Oddly, it is man who feels lost and alone on this planet, man who must live with a question mark suspended over his head. Is there anything to hope for? Anything to live for? Anything worth dying for? No easy answers are available to the best human mind. Man is a mystery greater than the stars; he alone is needled by the irritants of uncertainty. For he alone can reflect and repine, can sink into despair beyond hope of recovery. And yet he can know rapture, transcend the frontiers of the finite and move into mysticism. Man is the great amphibian. "What a piece of work is a man! How noble in reason! How infinite in faculty!" exclaims Hamlet alive with ecstasy. Then his dark conclusion. "And yet, to me, what is this quintessence of dust?" Finite and infinite, dust and divinity! Truly, man is the first mystery.

Man afraid

Man looks at himself and makes an inventory of his talents. He has much in common with the animal, its need to eat and sleep, its urge to procreate and survive. But he finds within him other impulses unknown to the animal. He is aware that he can choose, to eat or to abstain, to procreate or be sterile. He can disown life and choose to die by his own, ingenious hand. Man is conscious of himself; this impales his difference. He can experience joy of rare intensity. He can feel guilt and remorse. He can talk of good and evil. He is burdened with decision. The animal forages in familiar territory; it is at home by the riverbank or in the woods if its physical needs are answered. It is man who feels lost, the earth's only exile.

> "I, a stranger and afraid,
> In a world I never made."
> (A. E. Housman)

This couplet is the voice of the lost and lonely. But there is another voice. The masterpieces of human genius in stone and paint, in rhyme and music remind us all that his aspirations are not vanity, nor his creations trivial. The saint and the artist reveal man as more than man, his soul lit with grace and fired by some power more sublime than the lust for gain or the pride of possessions. This force is faith, a Reality more real than common things, more honourable than accumulation, more enduring than the toil and trade imposed by daily necessities. Yet only one thing is necessary. Each man and each woman is burdened by decision. Each must have an object. On this not something, but everything depends. The hedonist believes in maximum pleasure. The saint says "I believe in God". And we all wonder what exactly he means.

Interior conflict

What dominates your consciousness; that is the object of your faith. The thing you select as the one thing necessary reveals your god. There can be only one true object of faith, one good, one God. But there are many counterfeits on the market, all prettily packaged, all promising the good life with minimum endeavour. The mind names the one thing necessary as the Truth. The heart calls it the Good. The unaided mind cannot reach the truth. Nor does the heart by instinct opt for the good. For what we call consciousness is limited consciousness; and what we call awareness is reduced awareness. We live under low cloud and are held by fears and phobias that dim the horizon. We may not believe what we think we believe; we are our own best deceivers.

The world is now aware that consciousness is not a single-storeyed edifice, but has many levels. Dreams, fantasy, reverie emerge from below the rim of consciousness and tell us strange and terrible things. We are aware that we are divided; we experience that divide in conflict of self with self, and this can be the cause of neurosis and break-down. Two objects may be in contest for our allegiance; faith competes with faith. At the level of consciousness we may desire health. Yet, below, we may seek illness as the only access to care and alleviation. Or we may believe and speak as though we admire someone, yet, deep-down, nurse a strong contempt for their person and an envy of their success. This corruption of consciousness is the worst disease. Here no man or woman can be their own physician.

A little hope

Corruption of consciousness is a universal taint. No man, no woman is immune to its infection. As we grow in years and are hurt by the insults of experience we learn a hard lesson – that no one is reliable. "The best lack all conviction", laments the poet, "the worst are full of passionate intensity." This defines the human condition as lamentable, and, like Dante, inscribes an epitaph over the gates of the world. "Abandon hope, you who enter here." Yet, we enter with hope. We go in search of Someone, somewhere, who carries within him the secret of salvation. We cannot believe that this world with its order and intricacy is a doomed and forlorn place. We cannot believe that human heroism is sham, that the creations of human genius are no more than dust.

Christ speaks to this little faith within us. He does not deny that every heart is soiled and often sick, almost to death. Yet he affirms that the heart is a temple, not a tomb, and, though defiled, can be purified and become a sanctuary where God is pleased to enter. Yet, so conscious are we of our corruption, so ashamed of our sin, that we shy from God as from a fire that will consume, as from a light that will betray our most sordid secrets. This is the fear that contends with faith. Not fear of the dark. But fear of the light. It is not the dark men fear most. Obscurity is good cover and provides asylum. It is the light that men fear, the truth that men oppose, the good that men resent.

12

"I believe in God" is an act of return; a return to the light. There is no experience so exhilarating, no joy so uplifting as to witness this recovery of heart and hope. For recovery it is, a total restoration of a man or woman who had lost their hold on things and saw nothing but night and impending annihilation. The Gospels are tessellated with stories of people broken by the weight of adversity and, at a word, strangely restored. Bent reeds, flickering candles, lost sheep; these are the images Christ employs to reveal that we are all walking wounded, yet never beyond rescue. Peter disowns Christ, yet the coward is made the leader. The prodigal squanders a fortune in the stews of the secular city and returns to be received like royalty. Saul sees the light in a blinding flash and is forever changed. The persecutor becomes the apostle. So curious is conversion. So miraculous.

Judas worries us, saddens us. Like us all, he betrayed Christ. That was not his sin. His fault was refusal to seek forgiveness from the well of forgiveness. He could not believe that God would forgive his treachery. He turned away from the light, when he should have turned towards it. He tried to buy forgiveness, first with gold, then with rope. He did not believe in God's benevolence. And this is unfaith. The wages of this sin is death. Unfaith disables God. Here is sin at its most lethal. Here the malignant cancer and the terminal disease. Not moral transgression nor legal infringement make the malignant cancer. These are consequences of a more radical disease. Sin, at root, is unfaith. "He who believe in me has everlasting Life." Faith is the affirmation of the living; unfaith the stone heavy on the heart of the dead.

FATHER ALMIGHTY

If God is the Light, the fire which warms but does not burn, if God is the answer to the ache of the heart, then why do we not turn to him as flowers lean to the sun? Is there in us some impediment, some inhibition that makes us afraid of this inclination?

We fear God only because he is Holy and we defiled. This fear is congenital yet is not unfertile. Indeed, fear is the first grace and moves us to obey God's commands. Our observance is imperfect, our obedience fickle. Yet, in seeking to walk this way we learn a singular truth; that the commands of God are not imposition but the laws of our own welfare. To obey God does not diminish personality; it enhances it. Wisdom is budding within us. It is not the wisdom of the worldly-wise, nor of the cunning. This wisdom is the first-born of fear — the fear of God, and is an agent of maturation.

The fear of God is the first access to the Holy and imparts awareness of a Reality antecedent to known realities, beyond, above and below them. It is experienced as power and as presence. A strange power for it both attracts and intimidates. It is beyond our control so we call it transcendent; it is within our experience so we call it immanent. We cannot think God; only contemplate him. If we let him, in silence and seclusion, irrigate our consciousness, fear is transformed, dimly at first, dimly but really. We perceive that God is not threat, not frown and disapproval.

He is good and we may even learn to love him. Fear remains, for we are not God. But love is born of this dark question as the sun and the daylight rise from the night.

It is the distance of God that deters; his seeming indifference. A sky-God is so remote; God in a palace so aloof.

> "Your chilly stars I can forgo.
> This warm, kind world is all I know."
>
> (Wm Cory)

Jesus is unique in so many things. Not least in his manner of address to God. He calls him "Father". This is not an alteration of style. It is a revelation of the character and quality of God. The word "God" is cold and cuts a lonely figure; a divine bachelor, an infinite egoist, engrossed in his own perfections. The mind may accept such a god as it accepts a far-off galaxy. But the heart is not warmed to love or to worship. Who can compose a hymn or pen a sonnet to an unmoved mover, or a celestial architect? The god of the mind is ice for the heart. For man is not primarily a mind but a heart. It is love not logic that makes the world a place of poetry.

But with the word "Father" Jesus speaks not to the mind alone but to a more melodious instrument. He speaks to the imagination. Most of us are not trained thinkers. Few can manage metaphysics. Yet we are all moved by metaphor and imagery, and the great truths come to us in the colourful alphabet of the image. "Shall I compare thee to a Summer's day?" writes Shakespeare. "I am the good shepherd". So Christ describes himself to peasant and fisher folk in a land where sheep pastured among the high rocks, and a good shepherd saved them from the wolf. Religion is poetry rather than proof. And great poetry is love-poetry. If religion is reduced to the algebra of the mind, then its fire is extinguished. We are left with ashes, almost too cold to re-kindle. Our first access to reality is through the imagination and the child's first word may well be "Mamma". Or "Abba", Father.

Futurity

Jesus' first word is "Father". It is also his last. "Father, into

16

thy hands I commend my Spirit." Indeed, it is hard to open the New Testament at random and fail to see the word "Father". For the New Testament is a love-story and the love that gives it fire and inflammation is the affection of the Son for the Father. For Jesus does not lead a life of ease and exemption. He is not born in a royal creche nor lives in silken surrounds. His only coronet was made of thorns; and his death-bed a tree of torment. What sustained him in a pilgrimage, paved with sorrow, was not stoical endurance nor indifference to death. He was sustained as we are all sustained by a love that was stronger than the malice of men and the sting of suffering. Only love has this temper. It gives the soldier courage in the field and we see it in parents sacrificing for children, teachers for pupils, nurses for patients, and men and women for the undeserving and the ungrateful.

The Fatherhood of God is a revelation we do well to ponder. For Christ does not claim to be the point of our pilgrimage. His word is the "way". The way to the Father, the road to the future. None of us can live without a future. We need some vision, some light to attract. It may be marriage or money. Sadness falls when the future becomes the present. The marriage may not meet expectation, nor money be blest with magic. Then we are without a future and the light leaves our eyes. Jesus reveals the Father as the future and the fulfilment. This future is present in Christ. Yet it remains future. The Father is revealed in him and revealed as Love. He is also concealed. We do not see the Father by direct vision. Not immediately; but mediately. Jesus is the mediator of the future. And he dwells among us. But where? In people, in those who have a courage to see God with a child's eyes, and can with confidence say "Our Father". Faith takes courage. So obsessed are we by our sins and shortcomings that we fear to come too near to the light; it may betray us. Or too near to the fire; it may singe us. Christ reveals that this timitidy can be overcome; it is not humility but pride. We are not called to be God's satellites, not cringing servants. Our calling is high; to be sons and daughters and to see ourselves as loved without conditions freely, divinely.

Call is the crux of Christianity. We hesitate to answer. Christ is aware of this diffidence, and does not ask us to advance alone.

"Without me you can do nothing" is sweet consolation. To be Christ-like exceeds human capacity. We need to be re-born, to be elevated, to be Christified. To see with his eyes, to feel with his confidence. This is not difficult; only impossible. But "with God all things are possible." Even conversion from a sense of worthlessness to a realisation that God accepts me as I am and will lead me to a future which will answer my deepest ache.

There is fear in us all. A fear that if we become like Christ we lose our own personality. Not so. The more like Christ, the more our real self blooms and blossoms. The false self is the old pretender within us; he goes it alone. He keeps his distance from God and from men. He burrows within us like some nocturnal animal and yet craves the light. He wants acceptance; it is we who do not accept this shadow self and keep him hidden and battened down. But he beats at the hatches and rises in anger and rage and claims recognition. Acceptance of our darker self is hard but necessary. Faith is of the whole person.

The true God

Christ is total Son, with no reserved areas, no precinct marked "private". He is subordinate to the Father — "The Father is greater than I". Yet equal to the Father — "I and the Father are one". Subordination does not forbid equality. This is a truth that those in power are called to regard. How much suffering people would be saved if those dressed in authority did not employ it to dominate, to exploit and to subjugate. In God there is hierarchy without dominance; there is obedience without coercion. This is the kingdom we pray will come on earth; this is the power and the glory. Its name is love.

Jesus reveals that God is not a loner, not a monolith. The word "Father" is full of feel, warm with affection. This revises the natural vision of God. How fatal if we see God as infinite monotony, aloof, self-absorbed. But God is fire; in him there is heat and heart and desire. Desire to inflame, to re-kindle and re-create things numbed by dread of divinity. We cannot see the Father; the Light is too strong. Yet we are drawn to him as moths to a candle and cannot end this ache by substitutes, by men or women or money. The Father is the universal future, the magnet of all mankind. Yet we cannot see him, cannot know him. This is our pain. "Show us the Father". There is anger in this abruptness. Why will the Father not reveal himself? Why must we move and mourn in the twilight? Let us see the Light, feel the flame, know the future. Now.

Spirit

Jesus is the Light. But filtered to the vision of the human eye. He reveals the Father through a lens dimmed to our capacity. The time for glory is not yet; we have not the eyes. Here below we live on faith and faith sees through imperfect glass. Yet only faith gives access to the Father and a passage to the future. "No one can come to the Father except through me." Hard words and many cannot walk these evening fields, drawn by one single star. We want full glory, clear vision, instant bliss. Yet this is the dream; the fantasy of pride and impatience. Man is not God; his condition is human, his competence contained. To accept incapacity, that is faith in infancy. To aspire to transcend our incapacity, that is faith's adolescence. To find repose in faith, to know faith will one day die and vision come, that is faith mellow and mature.

Have we the energy for this slow ascension? We have not. "Without me you can do nothing" denies autonomy. There is a listlessness in us all that makes prayer and the practices of piety often so wearisome. Only in Christ do we see consistency, a faith which can contend with every adversary, with rejection, loneliness, and disappointment. Even his opponents perceived that a spirit burned within him that they could not submerge. They called this power demonic; a devil possessed him. Yet devils upset and divide and destroy; they are soldiers of sin, terrorists of the timid heart. They shriek and shrink from Christ for the unholy cannot abide even the presence of the Holy. Yet they have power; they can drive men to death or dementia. We see their signature wherever we see inhumanity. For holiness and humanity ride together.

19

Jesus does not deny that he is possessed. The Spirit is so strong that it goes out from him as heat and radiance and cannot be earthed. It heals, it makes whole. It gives peace to the anxious, love to the lonely, forgiveness to the sinner. It unifies. That is its function. Sin glories in divide as the psychopath glories in destruction. Love unites, heals, makes whole, makes holy. Indeed, we do not see love except through signs; the hand-shake, the caress, the kiss. Every kiss is a kiss of peace. And the work of Christ is to repair, to do battle with divide. Divide among peoples, divide among sects; above all, with the divide in me. We experience sin most poignantly through interior conflict. We have not the instruments of cohesion. I want to do good; only good. And yet, the evil which I will not, that I do. This is sin crying from the deep. It is a cry of despair.

The Spirit in Christ is the source of that sure-footedness which guides his steps through a landscape pitted and ploughed with treachery and chicane. Yet he stayed steady. In his sunset days he disclosed a divine intimacy. The source of his steadiness was the Spirit. Not human force or animal vitality. This Spirit is the agent of unity between Father and Son; it is eternal and enduring. And it is love. What is love, the world asks. "God is love" is the only answer. What does love do? It unites, gives peace. The peace-makers, they are the true sons and daughters of God. This is the bread and wine of revelation, not human inference. The best human mind cannot define love. The mind has not the reach to go so far. It cannot reach God. God must reach man. And man sees God only in one experience; the experience of answered love.

Connecting

We see God then, not in the stars, but in a true and deepening relationship. How much pain there is in a broken friendship, a fractured love. How much joy in a relationship which endures and grows and ends in mellowness. God lives in relation and we are made in that image. We cannot disown that impulse to connect and commune. The trinitarian God is the only bearable God, the God we can love and relate to. Any other god is hard. Many carry in their subconscious a stern and stony god of endless demand and infinite reprisal. The revelation of God as love and totally relational brings release from this idolatry.

Jesus who reveals the Father, releases the Spirit. It is this given energy that confers on us the courage to say "Our Father". Now we can pray, and pray with Christ. We can let the Spirit sing through us and lead us closer to the Father. Faith grows, becomes less tremulous, less afraid of sin and sorrows. We learn to relate to God; in consequence we relate to people. For love of God and love of neighbour are not contending loves, but one, single animation. Indeed, man or woman cannot love by hard effort. Only those who are loved can love. God loves us first and his Spirit is the octane that can give the heart the trust to love without hope of reward. Christ is the manifesto of the divine largesse. Christ is the energy of the Spirit subduing the spirits of destruction. God is almighty only because all-mercy. Any other god is an impostor; any other love an oppression.

The reality of God

The Blessed Trinity is not a doctrine. It is a reality. It is THE reality. And the nuclear reality is relation. If man cannot relate then he can only repine in a lost and unlovely world. The doctrine of the Trinity is an attempt, no more, to put into words what cannot be put into words. The doctrine is tentative; the reality is glory. Not metaphysics but poetry is the language of mystery. The thinker can communicate a truth. He cannot communicate an experience. That is the work of the artist. Not through philosophy, but through liturgy and prayer and sacrament can we know the reality of God and that love which burns there like golden fire. At Mass we say "Holy, holy, holy". No one can say more. Neither men nor angels. Let us leave it there, for silence is the music of mystery.

CREATOR OF HEAVEN AND EARTH

A lady looked at a hazel nut and asked: "What may this be?" And it was answered thus: "It is all that is made . . . In this little thing I saw three properties. The first is that God made it, the second is that God loves it, the third, that God keepeth it."

In this simple observation, Julian of Norwich provides a compendium of the theology of creation. Only the mystic has such educated eyes, schooled to see all things as made, and as carrying the hallmark of their maker. How Jesus emphasises vision; how he laments our failure to employ our eyes to see not what is not there — but what is there. Genesis does not give us a chronology of creation. It gives us a theology. And its revelation is of totality; that all that is, is made, is loved, is sustained. Creation is continuing. We see it not only in the liturgy of the seasons, in the stir of Spring and the flush of Summer. We see it in the painter and the poet, in the scientist disclosing old secrets and finding new energy, or in some gifted leader bringing order out of chaos and peace out of confusion.

Genesis opens with a grim overture, a fearsome tableau of primeval sludge and slack water, the deadness of uncreation. People fear chaos and long for order and shape and regularity. This is the work of the Spirit, and there is applause, a kind of drum-roll as each act of creation is completed. Each succeeding achievement receives a divine salute. "And God saw it was good". The goodness of God has spilled over, the love of God has found increase in a new estate, and man is made its viceroy. God makes a deed of trust and man is his trustee. A privilege. A responsibility.

Man now partners God in bringing creation to completion. He has within him a capacity to promote or retard, to make or unmake, to increase or diminish. Love is the agent of increase; it creates and pro-creates and re-creates. Love has vision and sees in a hazel nut all creation in miniature. It sees the divine love in its creation, the divine beauty in its form. Creation is the artistry of love. The artist loves God's handiwork. Before he takes up his pen, or selects his brush, he is in love with creation and seeks to reveal to unseeing eyes the infinite condensed in the finite, the hand of God in a Winter landscape, or in the face of a child.

Love is unafraid of risk. God hazards much when he assigns this great, big world to man's tenantry. Indeed God rates man more highly than man does himself. And this assignation seems like folly equal to Lear's when he resigned his kingdom to the care of his daughters. Yet God does not leave man unaided even when he betrays his trust; creation and redemption go hand in hand. The partnership is not broken but reinforced. For the fidelity of God is most moving when man is seen to be unreliable, unworthy of trust, without gratitude, inconsistent. God believes in man even when man falters in his belief in God. He is aware of that arrogance in man which seeks to make his lease a freehold, when he calls the world his oyster from which he can extract the divine pearl and make it his own possession. There is in us all a smouldering resentment at our status as creatures, depending for every heart-beat on a given impulse, for every breath on a given inspiration. Man envies God and would take creation from him and be lord in an atheist empire. "Better to reign in hell than serve in heaven." Satan speaks for us all.

Reverence

"I believe in God the Creator of Heaven and Earth" is both a truth and a prayer. The truth sets us free from the illusion of living in a God-forsaken place with no light or leader through the traffic of the world. The prayer is for the eyes to see all things as given things and our life as more precious than what we do or make. "The life is more than the meat, the body more than the raiment." This is not clear to envious eyes. There are so many pressures to live on acquisition and to see this earth as no more than a container of petro-chemicals to minister to industrial needs.

To see the world as God's world is a true reading and brings reverence for creation. Yet reverence now seems to be the virtue of a minority. A train journey through industrial England reveals how grim and grey things become when man sees the world as his possession. Streets huddled together in midget rows, airless houses, people crowded like battery hens and their lungs polluted by the smoke of adjacent factories. Many houses are now demolished and high-rise blocks slot the slum-dwellers in tall erections like filing-cabinets where many fret and are forgotten.

When the world is no longer seen as a sacred place, then man is devalued and degraded. He becomes a utility, a hand, a unit of production. Belief in creation saves the world from the deadening principle of utility. If everything is measured by its usefulness then man is just a consumer and the world a shopping precinct. People lose their taste for simple things, their eyes become envious and their hearts unhappy. Poetry is useless in terms of the market. So is art and religion. The good consists in goods; what matters is matter. This myopia is the disease of those who do not see God as creator and this place as his handiwork. Its outcome is anxiety; its signature, squalor.

Beauty is truth speaking to the senses. A sonnet or a symphony displays man at his most artistic. Yet his practical inventions, the computer or the electric cleaner are equally to be praised. The danger comes when man pays homage only to his own inventions and does not see God as the author of human ingenuity. The great scientist is a humble man and Einstein speaks of his "rapturous amazement at the harmony of natural law, which reveals an intelligence of such superiority that, compared with it, all the systematic thinking and acting of human beings is an utterly insignificant reflection." Only a great mind could have known this. Only a great man could have said it. The great are humble. They are the only realists. They reverence creation and their knowledge becomes wisdom; their emotion, wonder.

I BELIEVE IN JESUS CHRIST

"What is God like?" asks the child. We pause, we mumble because we cannot answer his question. For no one, not the saint, not the dreamer, has seen God at any time or in any place. The first astronaut, wheeling in space, derided believers. On returning to earth he said he saw no god seated on a throne in that spacious dominion.

A teacher I knew asked her children to draw God with their crayons. Their pictures were interesting, if somewhat disturbing. Both boys and girls depicted God as a policeman or as a soldier. In each portrait God was male, uniformed and authoritarian. Each of us carries a picture of God in our subconscious. And this God determines so many things, our feelings, our conduct, our prayer. And our happiness. Pious, church-going people are often not happy people. It was a child again — how much we learn from the child — who prayed "O God, make the bad people good and the good people nice." Strange that the professionally good are often so sour, so morose, so censorious. Of two evils they always choose both and their conversation is so often of calamity.

Two questions for ever tease and torment believers. What is God like? And what should man be like? Each of us is dimly aware that we are not what we should be. Not even what we can be. This is the heart-murmur of us all, a pain we call frustration. There is a gap between desire and achievement, between what we are and what we feel we tought to be. We read biographies of great people, of Florence Nightingale or Abraham Lincoln. As we read we are elated by their accomplishments. But when we close the book our admiration is darkened by despondency. They have succeeded. We have failed.

27

Where is the fault? Why do I fail? We blame parentage or bad schooling or the political system. Any alibi will do. But, deep-down, we know we are dissembling and that we cannot blame the stars. Abraham Lincoln was poor; Florence Nightingale a woman in a society masculine in its arrogance and attitudes. A quiet voice within us endorses the bleak confession of Cassius. "The fault, dear Brutus, is not in our stars, but in ourselves, that we are underlings."

The great African, St Augustine, was well aware of an interior anxiety which throbs within us all. "Our heart is restless and will not be quieted until it rest in thee." Yet how can it rest in God whose face none has seen, whose voice is mute or remote? No one can think God; no one can imagine him. The god we can think is too little; the god we imagine too flimsy. This is the impasse and no one can find exit. God must speak, must open and uncover and make the first advance. He must speak in a language we can understand, in an accent tuned to the common ear.

God speaks to man through a man. This is the only dialect congenial to humankind, this the alphabet of the learned and the illiterate. Men and women seek the true person by a strong impulse; there is despair when we cannot find him or her. Too often the leader becomes a tyrant; and the one who promised to be the saviour of his people becomes its seducer. History is the biography of great men and women. Yet, the historian concludes, most great men are bad men. Power corrupts more than gold. Great gifts are employed to pervert and destroy.

Yet we seek the good man, the true woman. We can do no other. Christ is the true man; only God could be. This is distilled revelation and here history is eternally altered. Our reading of reality undergoes total revision for God is no longer hidden but visible, no longer distant but near, no longer a notion but a person. From Jesus we learn that God and man are meant for each other as the lover is drawn to the beloved. There is no incompatibility between God and us, no broad ocean that for ever divides, no hostility that cannot be healed. This we do not learn from what Christ says or what he does. We learn it from what he is. Not a good man; there are many such. But the God-man.

The meaning of mystery

Great truths cannot be understood; only believed and quietly pondered. Such truths we call mysteries; they are the only interesting realities. Mystery is not the unknown or the unintelligible. Mystery is intelligible but also inexhaustible. The universe itself is mystery; we do not know how it began, how it will end. Its frontiers lie beyond our telescopes, its intricacy exceeds our understanding. We send satellites to explore planets within our galaxy yet know we have only deepened the mystery, not explained it. The stars keep their secrets.

Yet the mystery that touches us most intimately is the human person. What is his capacity? Is he more animal than angel, is he the crown of creation or evolution's most spectacular failure? What is his origin and what his destiny? Will he become extinct like the dinosaur or rise to the heights of mysticism, break through the limits of time and repose on the heights of eternity? Briefly, what is man? Who can define him?

The answer is not a definition but a person. The mind can contain a definition. The person holds a mystery. Indeed, this is the attraction of persons, their unknownness, those actions that surprise so that we say, "I never really knew her". Indeed, we do not know ourselves and we do things we never thought we would do — or could do. Introspection and self-analysis tempt us all. But so often all that they provide is more complexity, greater confusion.

How can I love?

We are not very old before we become aware that we are two people and torn by interior divide. "I am not myself today", we say, and so speak of interior contention. We love ourselves; and we despise ourselves. We love some people; we detest others. We are not in command of ourselves, not captains of our soul. For we want to do good. And we do evil. Not willingly, not wantonly. We want to love God and men with a wide, encircling love but are held by resentment and cannot snap its adhesion. Is this, then, the final condition of man and woman, the deadly dilemma? To want to love. And to be unable to love.

Perhaps we should begin with love itself. Statistics reveal that it is the thirty-sixth word in every song. The radio is alive with it. And do we know what we sing about? The lyricist who writes of the mystery of love shows perception. For mystery it is; the most impenetrable of all. It is the mystery of God. Everyone asks — what is love? And the Christian answer is brief. "God is love." This is the heart of the matter.

"God is love" subverts the accepted reading of love. We do not know what love is by human experience, by falling in love, and then predicate love of God. The truth is otherwise. Only those who know God know love. Much, then, that passes as love may be counterfeit. It is fashionable to talk much now of human relationships. But love is not a human attitude and cannot be engendered by whipping up the emotions, holdings hands and chanting of togetherness. Humanitarianism is not love; nor animal welfare nor any merely human altruism. Not that they are not admirable things. Just that they are not the real thing. They are not love. "God is love"; this is the nuclear revelation.

Those who know God know love. Yet how do we know God? Only by his self-revelation. And God has only one revelation — the person of Jesus Christ. Here love is traced to its origin and its origin is not found in the best man or noblest woman. Its origin is God; its manifestation is Jesus Christ. It is the great folly to presume that we know what love is antecedently and then attach it to God as a diamond brooch or glittering pendant. Not so. Love, then, would be a man-made thing. But there is no love of human manufacture. There is, of course, romance, and sentiment and appetite and passion. These make the themes of high drama, and fuel the heat of tragedy. But if we would know love we must know God. And God we cannot know except in his self-disclosure. And this disclosure is a person — Jesus Christ.

30

The optimism of Christianity rises like the dawn with this revelation. The morning comes and the night is ended and the sky bright with newness. Man has a fine future. His deep fear is the fear of God. To natural eyes God seems alien and aloof, not for us, but over us, even, at times, against us. At best he seems indifferent; at worst, hostile. Such a god is unbearable and makes atheists of us all. And such a god exists only in the diseased imagination. And every human imagination is diseased, for sin is eclipse and blots out the light; and we walk with uncertain steps. An American philosopher left home and lived in the woods just to think things out. He had reached a conclusion that he put in one memorable sentence. "The mass of men lead lives of quiet desperation." But why?

So much depends on the imagination. It is the imagination that sees ghosts and hears voices and makes for lunacy. It is the diseased imagination that makes god a monster eager to punish each peccadillo with great severity. "God", wrote Voltaire, "made man in his own image; and man has returned the compliment." This says it all. We project God. Christ reveals him. We project God from a heart sad and sick, too conscious of sin and contamination. There our image is moulded. If fear has dominion over the heart, then God must be fear amplified and made infinite. Inevitably, we lead lives of quiet desperation and this world is a desperate place.

Revelation is release. Revelation is new wine which asks for new wine-skins. And, let us not forget, revelation is disillusion. What we most need is to be free of two great illusions; two illnesses. Our image of God; and our image of man. No one has seen God at any time. We may add; no one has seen man, man in his integrity, at any time. The man we know, the woman we esteem are flawed by human frailty and touched by human weakness. Each one of us has been let down. We conclude no one is reliable. Sin is a virus to which there is no antidote and the wages of sin — death.

In Christ we see man in his integrity. We see the true man and he is worth a life-time's consideration. He is made of the same clay as ourselves, enclosed in human weakness, knowing all the shocks the flesh is heir to, traduced, taunted, rejected and doomed to die. He is not a super-man. Not a super-star. He is, simply, man. He is the norm, we the abnormal. He is the concentric, we the eccentric. He is the rule, we the exception. His life is not one of privilege and he asks for no exemption. He is not rich and he is not destitute. He is what man ought to be, Adam in his glory and Eve in her beauty. He is for real; we for illusion. Jesus Christ is the fully human.

Fully human because sinless. We learn from his person that sin is not what makes us human. On the contrary, sin is what makes us sub-human. Where we see envy and oppression, where we see whole peoples living in terror of prison and police, where we witness the pride of officials, the pomp of prelacy, the malice and meanness of common people, there we do not see man but his disfigurement. So pervasive is sin, so wide its circumference, so deep its penetration, that we settle for one sad conclusion — that man is rotten and beyond redemption. Not virtue, but vice; not good but evil, not grace but sin hold supremacy and make this earth a field of affliction.

Yet, if there is sin, there also is sanctity. If violence, also gentleness. If cowardice, also heroism. Which, then, is the true. Christ is the answer made incarnate. "I am the truth" is his unique equation. No priest, no philosopher speaks so serenely. Notice that "I am". Not "I have". This "I am" is the key that unlocks every door. "I have the truth" makes the truth a philosophy, a formula deduced by man's unaided mind. Such theories appear in almost every decade, a variety of -isms and -ologies. Communism and fascism, psychologism and sociologism; each in turn promises salvation. Yet all -isms become wasms and men look for yet another subject and a newer saviour. The newer, the truer — such is the slogan of our time. We equate novelty with truth.

For Jesus, the truth is not theory. He abhors abstraction for it is at one remove from the real. The truth is a person and only the personal matters. Not a book, not an explanation; it is a person who is the leading influence in your life. There is no sanctity in a system and no salvation in a syllabus. The heart and head of truth belong to the person and are as inseparable as light and sun, and heat and fire. Each of us seeks the true person and often despairs of finding him or her. The adjective "true" is wedded, indissolubly, to the noun "person". If we find this person we shall be forever altered. We shall be uplifted.

Truth is one; error multiple. Man naturally lives in error. Christ naturally lives in truth. From him alone do we learn the truth. The drama of his life is the theatre of the divine plan played humanly. It is not black theatre, though there is tragedy. It is not theatre of the absurd, though it does not march with human prediction. To the Greeks, who were philosophers, it was folly; to the Jews, who were believers, it was outrage. The death of God remains the great mystery and the last revelation of the love of God and the cruelty of men.

A look at sinlessness

The sinlessness of Christ answers, then, the question of the true quality of man. The true God is sinless; that we know. But we now learn that the true man is sinless. This is surprise. The more christified, the more human. The more human, the more divine. For Christ is no maverick; he is simply man, and does not disown descent from Adam but rather glories in his lineage. The fall of Adam happened in time and place and disordered history. Christ is born in time and place and reorientates the wayward course of things. In a sense, Jesus originates nothing. He redeems everything. The Christian prefix is "re". Renewal, revelation, reconciliation. Christ comes into a good world, wounded but well worth redeeming. He finds many good people, all sinners and unsatisfied. Yet seeking to be saved and believing that God will send someone, a prophet perhaps, who will be the agent of their release. He sends his Son as a cordial for tired hearts. A new horizon is drawn; it is infinite. People are made to be by gift what Christ is by nature — sons and daughters of God. No other destiny will answer the longing in every heart.

C

The people with whom Christ wined and dined, a motley gathering often of rejects and drop-outs, of the lost and the lonely, were alert to a strange power within him, a sureness, a faith beyond ordinary conviction. What was the secret of this peace which was the spell of his attraction? He reveals it in a sentence. "I and the Father are one." In him there was no interior divide, no nag of anxiety. He was one with his origin, not near to God but God without subtraction. We cannot echo this assertion but must say "I and the Father are two". Sin finds its origin here, in that feel of separation from our true origin — which is God. This is the root infection, this the original sin of which daily sins and repeated falls are the symptoms, the skin-rash which is the evidence of a deeper distemper.

Sin is not what we do. Sin is what we are. We do not commit sin and so become sinners. Rather, we are born sinners, so we commit sin. The child taken to the font is in a pre-moral condition, has spoken no angry word nor nursed any interior grudge. Yet is born in sin, in separation from its origin. It must be re-born and this it cannot do. God must come and call the child into a life not native to its heart. Baptism does not end at the font. It begins there. Baptism recurs. The course of living is not an easy walk on soft sand by an evening sea. Rather, it is a pilgrimage through a coloured landscape; there are peaks and valleys, mist and sunlight, night and day. Living is punctuated by occasions of crisis. Each compels response; a "yes" or "no". Illness, often nervous illness, comes to most. The illness is neutral; the response decisive. One may settle for a life of invalidism and its pleasing exemptions. Another may meet the illness head-on, fight, pray and overcome. The struggle is arduous and often long. But the day comes when he can take up his bed and walk into the world, his head high and his heart serene. He is the man of faith. To him Christ says "Your faith has made you whole". Grace has been offered and willingly received. The serpent of unfaith — the disabling sin — has been exorcised.

Sin is most eloquent in anxiety. Indeed, anxiety is the soil where sin roots and grows. Many people see anxiety as a little thing, a minor ache or itch. Christ sees it as large and as lethal. "Be not anxious" is no easy imperative. Indeed, it is a corollary of the first command, to have no false and phoney gods dissipating our attention. One thing is necessary. Oneness makes for peace; division breeds anxiety. We are given one pair of hands because that is all we need. We are given one heart but anxiety divides and disorientates it and we live erratically. Whatever we are doing, we feel we should be doing something else. This is not life but neurosis, not peace but suppressed panic. The devil is the author of divide and tempts us to seek the good life in glossy things that promise but do not fulfil. He promises instant salvation and it attracts like instant coffee. But there is no instant bliss. "Does the road wind uphill all the way?" the poet asks. And answers, "Yes, to the very end".

Growing up

The God-man is the true man; man in his integrity and man without anxiety. Each one of us needs security. Christ finds his in the consistent love of the Father. Everyone is called to maturity. Christ is guided by the Spirit, into the world and into the wild. He reveals the Father to give us our ground of security. He releases the Spirit to give us animation and maturity. For there is no life without growth. The leaf is the emblem of life on the oak and the dawn the recurring sign of the light that never leaves us. But the light rises and whitens the sky and though we sorrow at its setting we know this is the cadence of creation.

Christ, too, had to grow in stature and wisdom, in courage and understanding. He is not instant man but was perfected in that most comprehensive academy, the school of suffering. Man does not grow effortlessly like the oak but through a serial of dyings and risings. Rise, fall, decay, renovation, this is the cadence of creatureliness. At the age of twelve he died to the golden days of childhood. And not painlessly. Great questions troubled him; strong emotions stirred within his adolescent heart. Who am I? In a triduum of travail he prayed and argued. Then he emerged with but one, luminous conviction that God was the true Father, and his work the Father's work. This light would sustain him through wind and weather and lead him home by a road that passed through, not around, the traffic of the town.

Temptation

Christ knows each human experience. Not least, temptation. It is human to be tempted; inhuman to sin. The Spirit leads him to the wilderness for all temptation takes us into a wilderness; it is a symbol of the God-forsaken place. God loves a garden; the devil, the wild. Prepared by fasting, he confronts the tempter. And each temptation is subtle, each offers instant salvation. Power, prestige, possessions; this is the unholy trinity that seduces the secular heart. Instant bread, instant power, instant glory. And the price — to renounce the Father as our only future and fulfilment. To reject the creator and to worship creation. To disown God and to fall for money. Any man, any woman would fall for such enticements. Except one. The true man, one with the Father, totally free, wonderfully obedient.

The anxious heart is vulnerable and falls when offered easy money or good repute. Need is seldom the source of sin. The rich swindle; the poor are so often grateful for the pittance they have. Jesus sees no virtue in poverty; it is an evil to be remedied. But he sees danger in wealth. Indeed, his pity goes out to two classes and both are wealthy. Those who have money; and those who have piety. The affluence of gold and the affluence of virtue. Both sorts are in danger; both seduced to see salvation as bought.

The temptations of the pious are the most subtle and we need revelation to uncover this hidden heresy — the heresy of single-handed salvation. Whole pages of the New Testament burn with invective, with language of denunciation to lead the proud to a knowledge of their pride, the pretenders to a realisation of their sham and insincerity. The Pharisee does not belong to a time and a place. He is within every heart, the serpent that seduces even the elect. As soon as we begin to make an inventory of our goodness, we cease to be good. As soon as we begin to make comparisons, then we claim to be God. "Without me you can do nothing" must be accepted with a child's literalness. Evil we ascribe to ourselves; goodness only to God. The saint is not conscious of his sanctity, but of his sin. The mystic is unaware that he is a mystic. When Paul boasts he boasts in the Lord. "By the grace of God I am what I am." This is not the cry of Saul the Pharisee. It is the gratitude of the man who knows that grace is not bought, but a given energy without which we are unlighted fires.

Jesus pitied the Pharisee as he pitied the well-to-do. Without a sense of need, without experience of failure, without consciousness of sin, we have no hold on grace as the oxygen of every enterprise. A sense of need is a necessary anchor and grounds us in our condition of creatureliness. Creatureliness we resent. Humility is not what comes naturally. It is a long and arduous learning. "Learn of me for I am meek and humble of heart." Strange words from one who could command the wind and still the waves with a word. Humility is realism. It is humus, good soil and receptive to good seed and the source of growth and fertility.

Jesus Christ is man in his totality. Only God could be. Jesus has his origin uniquely in God; he is God. Yet, born of the virgin Mary, he is true and total man. This is the glory and offence of Christianity. For, conceived by the Holy Spirit and born of the virgin Mary, Jesus is not just near to God and resembling man. He is God-man. Oneness, not nearness, is the ache of the heart. And yet we fear to come too close to the tabernacle and inwardly desire to set some space between man in his meanness and God in his majesty. But the revelation will not allow us to screen God from man. True God, true man; these four words cannot be cut or conditioned to meet the limits of the human mind, simple or sophisticated. Yet that is human inclination. Great heresies train their artillery on incarnation. Either Jesus is God but only man in masquerade. Or Jesus is man and favoured by God. But not the Reality, only a replica.

The great mind

The mind of man is his glory and his pride. Yet, let us look at the mind. Let us first admit its limitations. True, it can set men on the moon and lift samples of its soil. But it cannot answer

37

the big questions. Why the moon? Why the universe? Why man? These transcend the capacity of the intellect; here the philosopher and the scientist must keep silent and stay agnostic. The genius of the mind is practical. It is to give order, to calculate, to cut to size. This is a necessary function. For there is simply too much reality. It presses from all sides and makes for confusion and threatens to overwhelm. Here the mind rises to the occasion. It tidies reality; it imparts pattern and design. Man needs order. The mind is both a corrective to anarchy and an agent of beauty. Order and beauty are precious things. But the mind is a filtering device. It achieves order by excluding great areas of reality to which we seek access, those rich pastures we call mystery and of which the poet speaks and the lover sings and religion celebrates. This is the estate of the heart and the heart has its own logic and language. It is not that of the mind, but more elevated, more nuanced, more poetic. This language is most moving in the psalms; they articulate the deep emotions of joy or thansgiving or wonderment. Both languages are available for human discourse. But the language of the heart, teeming with image and metaphor and comparison, is the language of daily discourse. The image is the currency of love and conversation. "My luve is like a red, red rose that's newly sprung in June." So writes Robbie Burns for he has no other language at his command. It is the language of love, the speech of the heart.

The mind resents what it does not understand. Hence, pride is the capital sin; it resides in the "caput", the head. The mind seeks to cut reality to its own capacity, to disown mystery and the realities it cannot reach. The mind wants total supremacy. It will not serve God or man; it will dominate them, be its own god and deny all mystery and refuse to reverence the hidden acres of reality. This Adam-instinct is in us all and Thomas is our spokesman. "Unless I see, I will not believe." Christ is our reproof. "Blessed are those who have not seen — and believe." We can believe what we cannot understand. We can believe in the God-man. Indeed, unless we believe we shall not enjoy the life we aspire to. And the great aspiration is for a life the best mind cannot engender. A religion small enough for the mind is not large enough for the heart. The mind cannot know God. Only love has the reach. And love is the blossom of belief.

The God-man is the ground of Christianity. Jesus Christ is God without reserve, man without sin or subtraction. The mind cannot hold these two facts in equilibrium for it sees all mankind as faulted. But the heart can be graced to assimilate more of this revelation. This is the way of the saints and this the hope of the sinner. Incarnation is total surprise, the great unexpected. We cannot argue to the necessity of Incarnation. Nor can we even envisage its possibility. We begin with the Fact. The Fact calls for faith; it will always exceed understanding, always offend the pride of intellect. The Christian mind is a humble mind.

Jesus is conceived by the Holy Spirit, the fine force of unity within God. It is now the force making him born of the Virgin Mary. Here a new unity is born. God is not just for God; but now also for mankind and its completion. The virgin birth secures the true godhead and full manhood of Jesus. Indeed, unity is the heart-ache of the world and the key to the Christian economy. The unity in God is pure wonder. But the unity of God and man in Jesus is sheer surprise. This should not be seen as the condescension of God, but, rather, as the elevation of his creatures. Mary is pure creature, purest of creatures, not subject to the unfreedom that sin imposes. She is totally graced, totally responsive to the divine energy, totally faithful. She says "yes" when mere human instinct would say "no". She says "yes" because she is free to say "yes". She assents to what she does not fully understand and so she is fully blessed. "Blessed are those who have not seen and have believed." True faith is immensely fertile; and fertility is the glory of woman. And true faith is active and its fruit is a new creation. God comes to Mary to seek her consent, and her acceptance joins the creature to God in the work of christifying and completing the labours of creation. It is the personality of Mary that is her first glory. God is drawn to her person, pure, innocent, virginal, and finds her wholly transparent to his light, wholly receptive to his call. Her "yes" discloses human freedom at its most spacious. She is free and willing and able to partner God in his noble work, and, in her, God joins the human race and the world finds a unity beyond its dreams. Heaven and earth are no longer infinitely distanced; creator and creature no longer eternally estranged. The son of God is the son of Mary and her consent is the word of reconciliation. The only word God seeks from us all is "yes". For where there is no faith God can work no miracles.

In her quiet affirmation Mary did not understand the suffering that would touch her. Nor did she see her maternity as a prize but as a responsibility. Hardly was her child born before she had to take flight from persecutors. Suffering was her companion; many things she did not understand. "Son, why have you done this to us?" is the lament of every mother. For there is no love on this planet so tenacious as that between mother and son. The Madonna and Child is the classic portrait of elemental love; the artist here meets the challenge of Incarnation. Perhaps its most moving emblem is the Pietà of Michelangelo where the dead Christ lies in the lap of the living mother. There is no anger on Mary's face, no resentment. Only the peace of one who believes that even this death has not fouled the plan of restoration, that the dead Christ has not died uselessly, that good and God will prevail. But how does she know? She does not know. She believes.

The fact of death

"For suff'rance", says Shylock, "is the badge of all our tribe." He was speaking to his own people, tried, tormented, exiled, ghetto'ed, and branded as infidel and heathen. Yet surviving. Not by evasion but by imbibing this bitter chalice. Shylock speaks for the whole world. For suffering is no mere incident, not a passing headache but the migraine of all mankind. A religion which is silent on suffering is a castle in the air with no foundations in the rough of reality. Theorists do devise airy constructions and seek to persuade us that our pain is illusory and can be wished away to vanish like smoke. But pain is not illusion, illness not always imaginary, and sin never without its invoice of guilt and remorse.

Even the merchants of illusion falter in the face of death. Death is so stark a fact, so bleak, so inexorable that it has a unique authority over the emotions. Like love, we do not understand it. Like love it is something we cannot conceal under the cream of apathy. There is no anaesthetic against the pain of bereavement; nor any elixir to prolong life beyond a given span. It is death that hangs a mark of interrogation over our best ambitions; death that makes men ask if life is not pointless labour and suffering useless expense.

Life is lived between the poles of love and death. It is love that makes for increase; love that longs for immortality. Every love-song speaks of immortality. "Thy eternal summer shall not fade." This is not poetic fancy but human longing, a faith in something that lasts and defies even death and dissolution. Only love has courage enough to believe in its eternity. Yet death comes to Romeo and Juliet, to Dante and Beatrice, to the saint and to the sinner. And death comes to Christ. This is the crux.

Hell

In his life, over evening tables, Jesus revises our understanding of God. He reveals God as one who cares and one who cures. This is not enough. Love does more than care and more than cure. Love is extravagant and always extreme. If God alone is love without limit he must show it. Death is his demonstration. Had Jesus not died he would not have been one of us. Had he been wafted to heaven and home, applauded by angels, carried on cloud, we would have admired and quietly despaired. For we would have been left alone with nothing save good example to remember, nothing save noble words to recall. And example does not save. It uplifts. And it accuses.

Jesus identifies. Where is the place of identity? It is the grave. To stand by a grave-side is to see all humankind as dust. Here both the great and the humble are equally degraded; here all are swiftly erased. The bouquets and the blessings, the archaic language of the obsequies do little to dispel the sombre conclusion that life at best is a brief and beautiful flirtation ending in heartbreak. In the green years, there was love and it was charged with immortality. It was a time for poetry, for song, for rapture and embrace. But with death, even the poet turns to cynicism.

41

The grave's a fine and private place
But none I think do there embrace.
(Andrew Marvell)

Such a pathetic couplet penned by a poet who could write so tenderly of love. But the grave casts its shadow even over the songster.

Jesus dies like any man. Few stayed to ease his agony. Rejection is the worst pain and he was rejected by man and abandoned by God. "My God, why have you forsaken me?" is pure pain and the line that lingers when we cannot speak our sadness and cannot abide our sorrow. This is more than death. This is hell. To be abandoned by friends is hard. To be abandoned by God is hell. Yet Christ did not despair; his faith remained even in this blackness and he commended his life to the Father who remained so strangely silent. The silence of God — how this oppresses the heart in agony. No pain so burns, no sadness so lacerates the soul. Jesus knew even this abandonment and could only cry his agony. But it was not a cry of despair. Faith does not despair even when the last lamp has been extinguished.

Jesus suffers every human experience and does not ride high over its pains and impositions. He submits to reality in all its rawness and does not super-impose some new plan which disregards the limits under which we labour. He is clay in the hands of the potter. He is a lamb obedient to the shearer. In a phrase that seems almost offensive, St Paul says that he became sin for us. But how did he become sin, he who was innocent of any transgression? He became sin by undertaking its terrible entail, the supreme agony of abandonment. The glory of love rests in a felt oneness with all things, with God and people. Sin is separation. It is experienced as lostness, as being out of tune with the harmony of creator and creation. Those nearest to God are most sensitive to the sin in the world. They see it as an oil-slick moving to defile clean and innocent shores. The godly are always most pained by sin; the vicious often unaware of its putrefaction. Only those who know good can know evil.

The Cross alone can be the symbol of Christianity. For there the two forces that touch us all met in contest. Love joined battle with death. Sanctity clashed with sin. And death seemed to win the field. He who claimed he was life was dead. He who, in a spectacular image said he was the Light, was quenched like a common candle. He who said he was the gate to life was shut in a tomb. Love, that wide generous, engaging love, which had drawn people to Christ like the starving to food, had lost its magic and its magnetism. On Calvary, sin — the author of death and divide — had its finest hour. Christ's best sermon on sin was his death. Only there can we measure its malevolence.

Sin is more than individual sins and St Paul sees the whole of creation as dislocated and labouring to find its form and completeness. And saints talk of the sin of the world as far more than the sum of individual failings. Only the saint has antennae sensitive to this universal contagion. Most of us are so preoccupied with our own individual shortcomings that we fail to see that there is in the world a demonic power that the most rigorous asceticism cannot overcome. It is also with this outsize sin that Christ is doing battle. It is this outsize sin which submerges him. He was acutely aware of this power and domination and saw its genius was concealment. The admitted sinner did not worry Jesus. For the Magdalens and the common sinners he had words of peace and compassion. It was those who denied they were sinners that provoked him to metaphors of intensity. Indeed, those who devised his death, would deny their work was malicious. It is clandestine sin that is most noxious. Only the saint can detect its tracery and only obscurely. Jesus could see it vividly and, in the garden, shuddered at its immensity. Battle was joined on the Cross. There sin registers its claim to supremacy. And it is written in blood; the blood of God.

Rising

But I hae dream'd a dreamy dream
Beyond the Isle of Skye;
I saw a dead man win a fight,
And I think that man was I.

Haunted lines. Strange dream of a nameless balladeer. Resurrection is no dream. It is hard fact, stranger than any dream yet prosaic in presentation. The Easter narrative is not lyrical but unadorned, austere in language, free of sentiment. For the Resurrection was not a spectacular event and Jesus did not come preceded by angels nor to a fanfare of trumpets. There was no sound. For Jesus is an apostle of silence and always a child of the night. He loves the dark and lonely places and the event which for ever alters the course of history is witnessed by none. The great ones of this world, the stars and super-stars, need pageantry and employ the organs of publicity to impress their audience and to reassure themselves. Jesus needs no reassurance. Never does he aim to dazzle by exhibition. He does not court popularity nor indulge in the deceits of display. He does not coerce; he persuades.

The drama of resurrection opens with an empty stage. There is no scenery save a garden, no light apart from the mist of early morning. There is no sound, only the silence that chills the heart when someone deeply loved and bright with promise has died. Indeed, the scene is one of desolation and, like a well-appointed grave-yard, it is a tableau of death. The apostles accepted death as the last curtain; it was the force against which all humankind was impotent. The miracles of Christ, the moving parables, the pastoral imagery, the metaphors drawn from the fields and flowers and sheepfolds, all were entombed in this grey garden. Who now recalled the seed dying in the soil and rising to make corn and bread for our invigoration? No one. Death alone has this power to congeal faith and to lead us to settle for apathy as the best analgesic to the pain of things.

Jesus respects human diffidence. He is aware that men believe in death more easily than in life, and that the faith which he comes to convey is not readily received. For resurrection breaks the sequence of cause and effect. It undermines all assumptions about the rhythms of reality. It is too large for logic, too elevated for common sense. No words Christ had spoken, no deeds he had done, disposed his followers to wait for his return or to expect it. For them, only one life was real. And Christ had lived it, gently, graciously, until that Spring afternoon when he was pronounced dead. They would mourn and revere him. They would not believe in him. He had fought and he had lost. But he had fought nobly. This they would remember.

Jesus had spoken freely about life. And "life" is an ambiguous word. For Jesus the life he lived in the villages of his beloved land was diminished life. It was a boxed-in life, a life of containment. It was short, hard and transitory. The Spirit burned strong in him but could find no outlet sufficient for its fire. The Spirit was willing, potent, reaching. But the flesh contained its power and impeded its elocution. His influence was real but inhibited. The Really Real, the life without limit, was not lived in Galilee. So he speaks much of the future and of a kingdom here but to be completed hereafter. This was strange talk and men warmed to its inflammation. But they did not understand. For he spoke of death in an accent of approval; this they found offensive. For them death is the impediment to life and increase. For Christ it is a grim but unavoidable depression in the climb to the kingdom.

Two lives

Calvary is, then, a cross-roads. The life before that summit is not the life to which the human heart aspires. It is life amputated and all who live it are paraplegics. It is real. But the life we dream about is the Really Real. The first life is a fever lacking the vitamins for health and happiness. And we do not pass from the lesser life to the larger by stepping-stones. The first life must be abandoned and this is not done willingly. It asks for courage, it asks for surrender. No one is exempt from this dying. Not even Christ. He gave up his life in his prime and the field was won in Gethsemane. Agony is contest, human preference against divine asking. There is no more harrowing experience. "Not my will, but thine be done" is the ground of all prayer and the path to renewal. But it is surrender. When Christ died, he was denuded and had nothing. He gave himself away, and knew all that is meant by that bleak word "abandonment". He had lost followers, friends, repute and the felt presence of the Father. He had lost all that seems to make life worth living. He had descended into hell and hopelessness.

The Creed does not state merely that Christ rose from death but also from hell. This is not a kind of primitive mythology but a truth; one that makes us free. For the worst pain in life is loneliness and death is a lonely experience. Loneliness comes to all and there is alleviation in company and distractions. But loneliness makes us afraid and it is this fear that moves us to seek human consolation. But there is a radical loneliness that no friend can mitigate, a total abandonment that is both death and hell. And this is unbearable. For it is not good for man or woman to be alone. It is evil. It is hell. The great pain of Calvary is not physical. It is this total exposure, this radical abandonment. The deepest fear is the fear of hell. Here man is totally lost, totally alone.

Total loneliness

For the Jews death was absolute loneliness and its name was hell. Christ entered this dark dominion where there is no voice to comfort and no hand to hold. When man has passed beyond the reach of love he is in hell and this is the only horror that destroys. Many a person can say with truth "I am going through hell". There is no word to substitute for "hell". Christ identified with man in this abandonment. He descended into hell. And he found exit. He entered hell to destroy it. He died alone that we might not die alone. He made death no longer the descent into total solitude but the avenue to life and enlargement. The only hell man can now know is pre-meditated and chosen isolation. This is not uncommon. But, as St Paul tenderly writes, "those who are in Christ Jesus are not condemned" (Rom 8, 1). Such sweet reprieve from a fear which infects the heart too conscious of sin, always living in dread of final rejection and eternal isolation. Jesus entered this hell and it could not hold him. He was raised and we are the beneficiaries of this release.

Resurrection, then, is no past event. Calvary is history; Jesus died once and for all. But Easter is contemporary and its tense is the present tense. "Jesus IS risen." And, if Jesus is alive, he must live somewhere and his only home is the human heart, always sinful and often sad, yet kept from the edge of total rejection. It is void that the heart fears, the emptiness, the loss of grip and identity. To be nobody, to be superfluous, overlooked by God and disregarded by people, this is to die even when living, to be alone even in company. This is hell already here. And this is unbearable. Jesus cried his abandonment and it is the voice of us all. He descended into hell. And he was raised.

Fear of rising

Yet few totally believe in resurrection. This is odd, for people often wish they had known Christ and dined with him and walked the evening shore beside him. How wonderful to have heard his words, to have felt the touch of his hand, looked into his kind and compassionate eyes. Yet his words were often violent, his hand once held a lash, and his eyes sometimes blazed with accusation. Christ had not come to condemn. Nor had he come to console. He had come to change. "Repent" is his first imperative. And "repent" is radical change, not superficial reform. It asks for a change of attitude, for new values, for something more than a routine practice of old pieties and a nervous attention to rubric and regulation. It asks for conversion from the real to the Really Real, from old to new. It asks for a dying. And for a resurrection.

Resurrection is fire and we fear its temperature. It is challenge. Challenge to what? Challenge to sameness. For Jesus the only signature of life is growth. And man does not grow effortlessly but only by a recurrence of crises often so harrowing that each seems to return us to hell. The great characters of tragedy are outsize figures and they magnify the dark experiences of us all. Hamlet is a soul in torment and sees life as hell and wonders if death merely intensifies present torment. He is a man without hope; no lamp is lit for him. This is high tragedy and we are spared its experiences. Yet we ask his questions and look for answers. We believe in death and in hell. We seek to believe in resurrection for this is the truth that transforms. No other. But to believe in resurrection is rare. It is the faith of the fearless. And most of us are afraid. This fear is no little thing. It is faith's great opponent.

It is fear that makes men seek cover in the status quo. The status quo, the idolatry of the past, the congealing of the present, these screen us all from the Christ risen and alive. To believe in Resurrection is to see life as growth. To disbelieve is to see life as repetition. Repetition makes little demand. It is safe, a daily sedative. And it is dead. Let the dead bury their dead, says Jesus, but we decline. So we celebrate Easter as a past event, an epilogue to a bizarre story, but locked in the archives, part of the record. We assert that we have the faith but the world wonders at our inertia and sees the Church as dead, a Gothic enclave in a modern thoroughfare. Yet faith finds its only focus in Resurrection. "If Christ be not risen all your faith is delusion", says Paul. All. This disturbs. Resurrection must disturb. It allows us no status quo, no lay-by on the pilgrimage of the present.

A remark made by Tertullian is commended by scholars for its insight. "Christ", he said, "called himself truth, not custom." Truth is a tree and grows. Custom is creosote and protects. Truth is of God. Custom is a human thing. Truth is fire. Custom refrigerates. Custom can be a good servant but a dangerous master with power to kill by kindness. For custom is kind and absolves from the need to think, to experiment, to innovate. Most men fear thought and are reluctant to take a new step. And their best court of appeal is custom. Yet custom itself was once innovation, and the past cannot be the determinant of the present. The gospel is news which must stay news. Or it too will lose its vitality and become a quarry for texts that seem to endorse the status quo. "You have heard that it was said of them of old" says Christ. And then his great offence. "But I say to you." And this remains his tense; the present. For the risen Christ is always present tense. Only the fearful make him past and do not hear his voice saying "Behold, I make all things new." This is resurrection-language and not the vocabulary of custom.

The Jews like every old nation were deeply attached to custom. They venerated the law, took pride in the Temple, and kept the Sabbath. Law, Temple and Sabbath composed the regalia of their faith and the cohesion of their society. All were endowed with immortality. They were as old as their sacred hills and were blessed things. Yet, Jesus came to complete the law, to replace the Temple and to substitute the Sabbath with Sunday — Easter Sunday. Here custom surrendered to truth. Here was change from shadow to Reality. And here, strangely, was love. For truth and love are one and admit of no divorce. Christ is its temple. He is alive and he is love. He respects the customs of the Jews and venerates the temple. But the life before Calvary is not the life he had come to relay. It was overture to something fuller, something finer. Christ too had to undergo change and it was not painless. The risen Christ wears the wounds of human brutality and does not complain of the price. Love does extravagant things, and truth is always lit with surprise.

So we see resurrection where we see life and increase and creativity. It is the genius of love to create; the desire of death to destroy. This is the only war, its field is the human heart. Resurrection is a new creation and the risen Christ imparts the impulse to create. We are called to co-create and to increase the sum of being. The symphony and the sonnet are resurrection-things and are born of the urge to explore the beauty of creation. Art is not first a technique but an inspiration and the writer may find he writes above himself and the painter learns from his own landscapes. Some spirit possesses and empowers them. It is the Spirit of God.

49

SPIRIT OF GOD

Personality

Common people sensed in Christ a power we call personality. He was animated by an electricty that went out from him and lent heat to the heart and healing to the dejected. So strong was this influence that people asked "Who are you?" They divined that he was more than a carpenter. His wisdom was deeper than that of the wise. He carried an authority more persuasive than that of their officials. His courage was equal to any circumstance; he walked steadily no matter how steep the path. This Spirit is not genius. He admitted he was possessed by that Spirit we call holy; the Spirit of God. When he died he released this Spirit, not to the winds, but to the world. He gave it to all willing to receive its animation. "Receive the Spirit" is his command.

The glory of creation is the person, the man or woman who is a real and rounded personality. Such people are rare, rare as rubies and as precious. Yet how they uplift our drooping spirits, how they convey the sheer goodness of being alive. They are people deeply in love with creation and see it as white with the sheen of promise and possibility. We seek their company; their very presence is a cordial. Their words bring peace, their silence serenity. "Blessed are the peace-makers" says Christ. Peace-lovers are two a penny, but peace-makers are the only aristocracy. We know them by their poise. Success does not make them heady and failure cannot ruffle that interior pool of quietude. One wonders what is their secret. For they are found in every condition, among the well-to-do, among the deprived, among the healthy, among the terminally ill. What is the spark that makes them a light to us all?

Simply this. They have died. They have surrendered the self that seeks to live in isolation from God and man. So much of sorrow and all of our anxiety derive from interior divide. One area of us lives under shadow and we do not admit its existence or allow it to see the light. Yet it is part of our composition; it speaks in dreams and fantasy. It inhabits the cellars of the soul and, though suppressed, is real and demands recognition. It is experienced as interior rage, as smouldering resentment. It is at odds with the conscious and speaking self. Yet it is not the evil within us; the evil consists in its suppression. This separated self only asks for air and admission for it too is God's creation. Divide is disease, wholeness is health. And we are diseased. We are called to health and to healing. But we cannot be our own physicians. We need a healer, one who accepts us as we are, in sin and separation and in sorrow.

We must die to the condition of interior warfare. This is not easy. We feel if we open to God totally we shall be totally destroyed. We keep the separated self as collateral for our comfort. We give the churchy part to God; we preserve the secular for our own purposes. So each of us is a divided house and a divided house cannot stand. Jesus comes to give us a standing and asks us to surrender not part of us; that is easy. He asks for something unique and terrifying; a total commitment, a baptism by total immersion. He does not underplay its price. He calls it a dying. And dying it is. Dying to autonomy, to the pride of egoism, to the illusion of self-sufficiency. "Without me, you can do nothing" is, by far, his hardest saying. Few ever accept it. But those who do are the real and rounded people. They have died. And risen. This is what baptism is about. It is a dying, death by drowning. It is also rising. We are naturalised into the rhythms of the real.

Jesus saw his death and resurrection as a fearful baptism and wondered aloud if his followers could accept it. They were people like ourselves, wanting prominence in the coming kingdom. They were called to die to these naive ambitions, to see that the true kingdom was no political construct. We cannot blame them for their obtuseness. It is ours. They had to die to what the world sees as the glittering prizes. And when Christ died their faith failed; every death seems a disaster. Only resurrection cleared their eyes and rekindled their faith. Only then did the conduct of Christ and the tenor of his teaching catch fire and kindle their hearts. Only then did they surrender and receive the Spirit. They remained Peter and James and John. Yet they were now other Christs for the Spirit which burnt in them was now Christ's own animation. They had died to the half-real, to the life of half-giving. They had risen to the real and Really Real. Only after Resurrection do we see the true Peter. When the cock crew he was dispirited. But, after Whitsun, he is a new man and his words burn with a fire that we recognise as inspiration. When Christ died, Peter died. When Christ was raised, Peter was reborn. There is no other way. "He who would save his life" — the life of completeness — "must lose it"; the life of partial giving. This is applied death. And applied resurrection. It is of universal application.

The Resurrection proves nothing. It reveals everything. It must not be employed as an apologetic. Indeed, Christ at the end of a parable made it clear that a man rising from the dead would not convert the agnostic. Resurrection is a fact. The only response to its authority is one of faith. There are so many death-things, so much disease and calamity, that it is common sense to see death as the dictator of human destiny. But those who believe in Resurrection are aware that life is the stronger force and that God is never mocked.

Ascending

Jesus comes to answer our big questions. Perhaps the question that teases and sometimes torments us before we sleep and the moment we wake is — where am I going? The child, its eyes open with innocence, does not find it hard to believe in heaven. Heaven is a place where people are kind and there are sweets galore. This fairy-land heaven dies when we become adults, when we sin and meet suffering, when we are let down, when we know rejection and our hopes are unfulfilled. Then people talk more of hell and many see life as an uphill climb against heavy odds ending in a cheap funeral. This is hell. Man is taken for a ride — to nowhere.

What, then, is heaven? It is a state and not outside our experience. After a wild Winter and too much worry, we may holiday in some secluded place with the company of a friend and find that the sun adorns each day with goodness and glory. We look for a word to describe this enchantment. We can find only one adequate noun — heaven. No other will do. For now everything is good, and life passes beyond the frontiers of finite things. Time no longer oppresses. Silence is sweet and conversation kind. In a word, we are transformed and our horizon has space and the world is alive with wonder. We are in love with creation, with stream and river, with man and God. For we are aware that this heaven is not our making, this experience somehow undeserved and blest with surprise; an ascension on given wings. Not our own elevation.

Heaven is the meeting of God and man. Jesus did not soar into space, folded in cloud. He went home. Indeed, in his last discourses, there is a note of homesickness, a longing for return. Love is longing; this is its pain. Every human love knows pain for it is incomplete. Every human love knows anxiety for it fears impermanence. The loved one may die or grow old. And if death is the stronger force, then love is illusion and man and woman should arm themselves against its attractions.

Ascension reveals that we are meant for heaven, that our imperfect love will find completion only in meeting with God. Jesus knew both death and hell, the crucifixion of the body and the pain of the abandoned heart. He was raised from both and he ascended. Man and God meet and there will be no parting. This is heaven and this is the term of ascension. Indeed, we understand heaven only from the ascension, not from the poet or painter no matter how ably they employ their art. The great truths cannot find expression for they exceed the alphabet of words. Music makes the best attempt. It remains an attempt. In the presence of mystery we can wonder and we can worship. We can join the angels and say "Holy, holy, holy". But we cannot fully understand what we say. Only God is holy and only God is love. We aspire to both and there is a desire for ascension in every love-experience. Ascension to completeness.

Heaven

It is good to note that Resurrection does not mean return to the common life, it is breakthrough to that larger life of which Jesus often spoke. He did not come back — like Lazarus. He went through. To a life not mortgaged to space and time, to pain or death. So we can never fully understand the risen Christ as our own lives are hampered lives and live with hindrance. And death awaits us all.

Equally, we cannot fully understand ascension. We experience it as desire for a larger life. We want to go up in the world. We pity the person who has gone down and become a derelict living on drugs to ease the pain of abandonment. We do not know what it is we aspire to, to which glory we are called, to which destiny we are driven. We call it heaven but cannot know its quality, yet it occupies our day-dreams. The ascension is ascension to heaven. And heaven can only be home and home can only be happiness. And the only happiness is to be loved without fear of love going into decay and dying on us like a spent candle.

Hell is total loneliness. It is one of two possibilities open to each of us. For loneliness is often self-induced. It is not absence of company. It is refusal to answer the call of God and the friendship of people. Hell has its attraction. It frees us from the demand that every friendship makes. It absolves us from concern, from receiving anything from anyone. It flatters our pride in being self-sufficient; owing no one anything. An instinct in us desires to live behind bars and to build barricades. A native pride in us does not want to receive. A native fear does not want to give. Hell is self-enclosure, and it is man's choosing, both his prison and his pride.

God calls all people to heaven. Jesus descends into hell to destroy it. He ascends to heaven to prepare it for our entry. Indeed, heaven is not some mansion previously closed to human-kind and marked "no entry". Heaven becomes real only when God and man meet and are at home. Heaven is not just God's apartment, plush and expensively appointed. This is to trivialize heaven, to make it folklore. Heaven is man's future fully realised. Christ is everyman and, after all the travail, he reveals man's future when man and God meet in full accord and with no fear of separation.

Hell is chosen isolation. Heaven is entirely the generosity of God. Man can make hell. God can make heaven. He makes it for man and the ascension of Jesus is the graph of man's future. Man on his own has no future and many of our contemporaries think too little of man and see him as a lost and wondering creature with nothing to hope for. Belief in ascension is seen as childish. Yet it is belief in man as born for greatness. Without a vision of greatness people cannot live and achieve. It was a prophet who said that where there is no vision the people die. He could have added — and descend into hell. Only two possibilities are open to man; hell and heaven. To choose isolation, to be deaf to every call to love and be loved is open to man. This is hell; this is descent. But to answer the call of God, to believe that this is a good world and that man has a future where his love will find fulfilment and be at ease with God — this is heaven. The saint experiences it now and can only stammer his experience. But even we have moments when we say "it is good to be here". Heaven is building within us.

TO JUDGE THE LIVING AND THE DEAD

Judgement frightens. We read it as condemnation. And life is intolerable if we walk under threat of rejection, in fear of condemnation. Christianity, then, is hardly good news but wild alarm. We live under shadow; our days are dark, our nights restless.

This is to misunderstand both judgement and Jesus. Remember how he lifted the hearts of his hearers by one fine assertion. "I have come not to condemn but to save." Clearly, for Jesus judgement does not mean sentence, nor is the day of judgement a solemn assize, a court from which there is no appeal. This picture, though portrayed by extravagant artists, is not the true picture. It is how men see judgement; a human recording. We need to recall that God's ways are not our ways, nor his thoughts ours. Christian truth cannot be inferred; only revealed. And revelation lifts the drapery that conceals the many-splendoured thing.

The key to this article of the creed is a pronoun — He. HE will come to judge the living and the dead. And this "he" is the Jesus who would not cast the first stone, who had tenderness for the failures, who did not despise sinners but dined with them. Possibly we are almost too familiar with these stories of mercy that we fail to register how little they accord with what we would expect. The pious were appalled, the priest and prelates enraged. Simon the Pharisee could not understand how Christ would allow a woman as notorious as Magdalen to approach him, much less anoint him. Yet Jesus did not retract nor murmur an apology. "Much is forgiven her because she loves much." Understand that and you see the finger of forgiveness. Forgiveness is the wheat-germ of Christianity. And it is hard to understand, as hard as love.

Forgiveness is not commonsense. Nor is Christianity. Commonsense would not receive the prodigal son like royalty. There would be no ring and no robe. There would be retribution. Yet the father judges the wayward son. He does not condone his sins nor overlook his extravagance. He looks for one spark he can kindle, one sign of repentance. He finds it in the only action the sinner can perform. This action is return. Repentance is earthed in return. No more is asked. God wants us back, wants us to believe that no sin we can commit can put us beyond the reach of God. This is hard to believe for sin has such weight, such nausea that it is natural to see it as decisive, a lethal injection.

One sin puts us beyond the hand of God. To see God as condemnation. Many do. The sin of Judas was not to sell Christ for money. His sin was disbelief in God as mercy. He did not return but retreated into the closed areas of the self where there is only the bite of remorse. We can never forgive ourselves. "To err is human, to forgive, divine." It is faith that releases a man from self-disgust and self-condemnation. The opposite of sin is not virtue. It is faith. And faith in God as all giving and for-giving. Faith is reply to his offer and advance, yet few can accept divine largesse. A native pride wants to level with God and achieve perfection by single-handed endeavour. This is not difficult; only impossible. With God all things are possible. Most of all, forgiveness. Forgiveness is the miracle and a total restoration. But forgiveness takes two. One who gives and one who receives. Unfaith disables God. He can work no miracles where there is no faith. And where there is no faith, we become our own executioners and die by our own shaking hand.

Day in, day out, Christ reveals himself as our brother. People afraid of God were unafraid of Christ. Children ran to him, sinners and the sick asked for healing, a criminal on the cross asked for forgiveness. God has commissioned Jesus to be our judge. Hence the joy of early Christians who shouted "HE will come to judge the living and the dead". No one else. This man who knows our condition by hard experience and is one with us in our suffering, in our trials, in our scorching temptations. He will be our judge. And no one has heard him utter a word of condemnation to a returned and contrite sinner.

Judgement, then, like all great experiences now undergoes revision and a new star is born. It lights the heart with hope. The day of judgement is a day of wrath only for those who turn from the light because they believe they do not need forgiveness and presume to be their own saviours. They believe they have levelled with God and dispensed with any need for grace, anything gratuitous. Indeed, they go on to judge other people. And their judgement is condemnation. They were Christ's daily heart-break for they were so bland, unconscious of any sin or shortcoming. They held posts of power in the church, they paraded their piety. They made religion onerous, for common people who had not their learning or literacy. They bound burdens on the backs of people and, for Jesus, this was a great perversion. Religion is meant to be a support, not a load. True, just being alive imposes a yoke and a burden. But "My yoke is sweet, my burden, light." How consoling. So heavy is the weight of sin that without the lift of forgiveness we should perish. Those who lean not on God but on their own virtue are agents of death and darkness. We cannot live on merit; always on mercy. Only Jesus is allowed to judge. And how kind, how courteous is his address to the returning sinner.

Self-judgement

God assigns judgement to Jesus only. "Judge not", is a serious command. Of course, parents must judge children, teachers must judge pupils. But these judgements must rhyme with the judgement of Christ. They must be ordained to save. The parent who is not angry with the child who refuses to do his homework does not love the child and cannot save him. If the parent is indifferent and allows the child to idle and drift, this is not good but evil. The parent is proxy for God and must judge as Jesus judges — to bring the child to the stature of which it is capable. Love is the only energy of salvation. Its opposite is not hate but indifference. Those who hate, also love. But the indifferent are dead; they have no mercy. They judge the world as lost and people as depraved and life as bad theatre. Jesus was appalled by tepidity. The worst disease is indifference. Yet even this is curable for those who turn to Christ for his mercy and his judgement.

"Judge not" asks that we should not judge ourselves. Many who judge themselves condemn themselves. This can be a serious impediment to happiness and spiritual maturation. To be obsessed by one's sin is not health but disease. For sin is not the primary religious reality. The true man is sinless. He asks us to be conscious of our sin but not to be overwhelmed by it. Consciousness of sin should be sheltered under the larger canopy of forgiveness. The saint is conscious of his sin. But he or she is more conscious of acceptance by God even if, on the surface, they feel unacceptable. The saint takes literally what most of us take only partially — that God loves sinners. This faith imparts enormous energy and is the secret of the saint's achievement. They have confidence. Not in their capacity but in the power of God experienced as munificence. For them only Christ is judge. For most of us self is judge. And this judgement is often condemnation.

To accept Christ as the only judge is to undergo a shift of consciousness. For our happiness is determined by what occupies the centre of our consciousness. We know our true concern by what comes when the mind is in neutral. The heart is dyed the colour of its leisure thoughts. Faith is not a better person but a new one. The religious person is so often sad because his consciousness is out of true. He judges himself and, try as he may, can find no sign of amelioration. "The truth will make you free" says little to him. The disease he suffers from is serious and not easy to detect. It is the corruption of consciousness. There is no worse corruption.

This corruption is not beyond remedy. It is evident when the thoughts we entertain are pessimistic, when we see no future for the Church or the world, when our best pleasure is in predicting calamity. We find no one to praise, but many to condemn. Cynicism is not a minor defect, but almost an anti-Christ. It does not judge people only. It judges Christ and subconsiously sees him as a noble failure. This attitude can be consistent with religious practices. Yet it is sin concealed and the more vicious for its concealment. Christ was aware of this cancer, which, if undiagnosed, can become malignant. He sees it as lived untruth. And no man or woman can cure it. The truth is the only remedy and always painful. And the truth is not a recipe or a formula. The truth is a person. "I am the truth". To allow Christ to possess the centre of consciousnness is to see all things differently and to hear a sweeter music. It becomes a lyric in St Paul and speaks through wild and engaging exclamations — "I can do all things in him who strengthens me. Rhetoric? Rant? Intoxication? No, simply, truth. Christ alone is judge for he alone is the Truth. Only the Truth can judge. And release. And save.

I BELIEVE IN THE HOLY SPIRIT

When Colonel Charles Lindberg flew the Atlantic alone in 1927 he called his machine "The Spirit of St Louis". We know why. He was not referring to the wood and metal that comprised his precarious craft. What made the flight possible was not the machine but the man. And what stirred the man to risk his life over grey and hostile waters was some deep impulse, strong and compelling; something passionate. We call this power by a word we cannot avoid. The word "Spirit".

It is an elusive word, a word with wings, and we cannot cage it; it is always in flight. Spirit is everywhere, for spirit is the genius in life. There is no spirit in a coffin; only death and rigidity. There is no spirit on the moon for there is no leaf or laughter. There is spirit where there is movement and maturation; where there is effort and enterprise. It is a compliment to say of someone that he or she is full of life. We warm to that person and seek to sun ourselves in the radiance of their personality. If sad, with too many sorrows, they uplift us. Each smile is a benediction, each word a release. Their very presence is a renovation; we know it is good to be alive.

Spirit attracts. It has magnetism. People followed Jesus into wild and lonely places for they were made new by his presence and made strong by his words. He spoke as no man had ever spoken and his speech was refreshment, it had the ring of truth. The ring of truth? What do we mean? Simply that truth has its own accent, an authority that gives meaning to lives without joy or direction. No glory can outshine the glory of truth. For truth does not inform. It changes. It transforms.

It is Jesus who discloses the fecundity of truth. "The truth will make you free." Golden words. For we seek freedom as a flower seeks the sun or the starving seek bread. And we are not very old before we realise that freedom is an interior thing. The young see freedom as release from the constraints of family and the restrictions of school. They dream of a room in the centre of the city with no rules, no impositions. They rent the room and soon sicken with loneliness. To palliate the pain they try new pleasures and loud company. These diversions bring temporary ease; the real wound remains open and untended. One can only pity their condition; drugs and drink merely intensify the loneliness. Freedom, they conclude, is a folly, just front and facade.

Yet freedom is man's right and birth-right. Dictators deride it; iron regimes suppress it. Only democracy has won for people the field where freedom can flourish and grow. Yet democracy has existed only for three per cent of recorded history and only in a narrow area of the globe. It is a fine achievement yet it lives under threat and, like a tree that takes a century to grow, it can be felled in minutes. The truth is this. The heart both wants freedom and fears it. Those who fear freedom are eager to take it from those who enjoy it. Freedom carries obligation. Its obligation is responsibility. Those who fear responsibility will trade their freedom to one who will live their lives for them. How unwise to assume that everyone wants freedom! The dictator climbs to power on the shoulders of the timid. He offers to undertake their responsibility, if they will surrender their freedom. And the police state with its labour camps and nocturnal arrests is born.

True freedom finds its home within. It is freedom from interior phobias and compulsions. Even in the best democracy there are many who lead pathetic lives, ragged with anxiety, because subject to the command of dark forces they cannot control and do not understand. Their hold on life is slender; their enjoyment of things non-existent. "Oh how weary, stale, flat and unprofitable are all the uses of this world!" Hamlet is their spokesman. It is not uncommon to become dispirited even while believing. The practices of piety may be a tedium, prayer may become perfunctory, sermons do not speak and the ears do not listen. Religion itself is arid and life a long and pointless labour. We cannot rouse ourselves from this unwanted sleep but are lost in lethargy. We are dispirited. The salt has lost is savour.

Only the Spirit can release us from this torpor and return the dead heart to life. Many who came to Christ had little hope. The load of sin and the weight of sorrow had led them to the edge of despair. They came to Jesus for they sensed that some strong Spirit breathed within him and they sought to inhale its fragrance and refreshment. In coming to Christ they did all that was necessary. "Come to me all you who labour and are burdened." Such a sweet command. Christ is eternal refreshment and the Spirit burning within him the one fire no power can quench. He is the salt that never loses its savour. It is from him alone that we know of the Spirit and find that its genius is to restore, to renew, to make alive. He does not call this spirit from the deep or invoke it from the air. It is within him, the fire of his energy and animation. It simply goes out from him like a radiation; merely to touch the hem of his garment is to be renewed. This Spirit is Holy. It does not destroy. It makes. It makes whole. It makes holy.

Conversion

The history of the saints is the history of the Spirit. They are not a superior caste exempt from the cares of our condition. They are sinners all, and they have known the agony before they have soared to ecstasy. Like us, they have known crisis. With Saul it occurred on a road. Saul was a deeply religious man. From boyhood he had been schooled by religious men. His special talent was for leadership. His fervour made him an exact and exacting exponent of the law. No man could have kept the Jewish law so scrupulously. His zeal for the law led him to pursue and persecute the first Christians. Yet Saul does not seem to have been happy. Zeal is never enough; it breeds bigotry. Unless tenderised by love zeal becomes destructive. Saul witnessed the martyrdom of

E

the young man, Stephen, and perhaps the gentleness and courage of that martyr made him think again about Christians and their Christ. For, on the road to Damascus, when God speaks he implies that Saul is not happy in his role of persecutor. "It is hard for you, kicking against the goad, like this." Saul, it seems, was a divided man. At the level of consciousness he was doing what was good. At a deeper level he was unsure. "Who are you, Lord?" he asks. "I am Jesus and you are persecuting me." No more was needed. Saul was released from an uncongenial role. Paul was born. The truth had made him free.

This is conversion and this is the work of the Spirit. No man can convert. The Church cannot convert but only prepare the soil for conversion. Conversion is the work of the Spirit and Jesus is its outlet. St Paul never tires of the wonder of conversion. Yet, he was religious before. Where lies the difference? Simply, in freedom. The Spirit had released him from a religion of law and regulation and led him into spacious fields where the Spirit blew fully and freely. Religion was no longer a burden but a grace; no longer exterior but a whole and healthy heart. How poetically he writes of the Spirit and the space and width of its generosity. How he feels for those for whom religion is reduced to legal exactness and neurotic observance. And how boastful he is. "By the grace of God I am what I am." But his boast is in the Spirit.

Deadness

The most damaging adjective we can attach to any man or woman is not "evil" or "bad". It is to say he or she is "dead". Evil can be made good; its sin can be forgivevn, its malice extracted, its power made creative. Great saints grew from great sinners. Yet not by endeavour alone. They received the Spirit and its energy imparted a new confidence and new courage. They were still conscious of their sin. But they could look on God and say, with confidence, "Our Father".

Deadness touches us all. It is a kind of virus that makes for indolence. We brood over our past and lament our present. We can see no future. Our conversation is a litany of complaint and our hearts a mush of self-pity. This is not living or partly living; it is a slow dying, a long and unlovely coma. To settle for this condition as God's design and man's destiny is to sin against the Holy Spirit. It is to choose hell and to glory in our choice. It is pride taken to the last decimal point, the sour grapes of resentment — that I am not God and things do not minister to my pleasure. So we create a narrow, airless kingdom where only "I" exist, and only "I" am important. It does bring a perverse satisfaction; hell always does. It is the palace of the proud, and the place of perdition.

Deadness is the anti-Christ. Life is the kingdom, the power and the glory. And life is given, not made. "All life, all holiness comes from you." It comes like rain on receiving soil, like the sun on the rose that opens to its invitation. The Spirit asks for openness; it is offertory, not invasion. We can resist the Spirit. We do. For there is, deep in the heart, a counter-spirit, a leader of the opposition, which resents God and resists his approach. The devil is no fiction of folklore but that hard area inside of us which claims divinity and denies it owes its life to a Creator-Spirit. We may not be aware of this demon; its genius is hiddenness. In characters of strength it emerges as defiance. "I will not serve." In most of us it is experienced as fear. "Depart from me, O Lord, I am a sinful man." Both want God and his goodness to dissolve. One man believes he does not need salvation. Another that even God cannot save him, so damned does he feel. Both resist the Spirit. Both prefer the prison of the "ego" to the fields of liberation. They find cover in the dark.

Darkness is lived untruth. Even for devout Christians the world may be twilight and the sun well below the horizon. To receive the Spirit is to see a whitening sky and to experience liberation from our worst fear — the fear of God. The Spirit enlightens the mind; it liberates the heart. Left to itself the mind cannot find the true God, only an idol, born of a diseased imagination. This pitiful parody darkens the consciousness of many people and makes them afraid. They may even want

67

sanctity but, subconsciously, resist the Spirit. Like St Paul in his violent days they may resort to legal exactitude and a rigorist piety. But, if open to the Spirit, they will be released from the false and find the true. They will not be slightly changed. They will be transformed. They will be reborn and a new light will grace their eyes. Fear remains, but not servile, not cringing. Only the healthy fear of hurting the one who loves them to distraction. The fear of a son, not of a satellite. The fear of a daughter, not of the damned.

The challenge of change

The closed mind is the mind closed to the Spirit. Such people learn nothing. Experience does not teach; they resist the insights of every new science, and live in the past which is their coffin. They may idealise the period of their youth and see everything that happens since as swift decline. They live on prejudices which they call principles. The Spirit blows no more and the present is total decadence. Yet the glory of the Spirit is its presence. It is an eternal wind; and always a wind of change. And change is its offence, for we fear change as we fear mortality; the one change the intransigent cannot avoid. Yet without a receiving consciousness there can be no progress. "To live is to change" wrote Cardinal Newman. "To be perfect is to have changed often." The insight of a spirited and spiritual man.

The closed mind Christ found hard to penetrate. But the closed heart was the mortal impediment. We cannot possibly understand the gospels unless we see on every page that much of the resistance Christ encountered came from the pious. Strict, moral, upright people. Pillars of the Church. But hollow pillars. They believed they believed. Jesus challenged their presumption. And for this he died. We cannot assess our faith by listing our devotions or counting our pious practices. Faith is a growing thing and it flowers as love. And the love of God is earthed in the love of people. They are not two loves but one single attitude. Where there is moral rectitude, there may be no love. And where there is no love, the Spirit has been refused. The heart is cold. And a cold heart is lived atheism. Nothing so distressed Jesus as those who professed to love God but cared nothing for people, for the lost and the lonely, the drop-outs, the sinners.

The love of God speaks through the love of other people. And it is hard to love people; many are unpleasant and some impossible. The successful we envy; the failures we despise. But why? Partly, because we have a concealed self-contempt and do not love ourselves. The successful man or woman is a standing judgement on our own seeming littleness. So we slander and denigrate. "He was lucky." "She had influence." This is untrue. And untruth is a jailer and confines us to the camp of our own complaining "ego". So many people are confined. Their conversation is composed of hard comment on friends and relations. They are prisoners of their own malice; poisoned by their own meanness. Jesus pitied their condition, for we are not born to slander but to praise. And if we cannot praise people, we cannot praise God. For he made them and he loves them. He wants nothing but their liberation.

How we all warm to that exceptional person who has eyes for the glory of things. How we are enlarged by the person who can admire. When we can no longer admire, we are already dead. Wonder, admiration, praise, gratitude — these are the emotions and make the best music of humankind. "The world is charged with the grandeur of God" writes the poet. But is it? So many see the world through bleared eyes and find nothing to admire, nothing to praise. For Jesus this is blindness. He gives eyes to the blind so that they may see some impress of glory on this bruised and bleeding world. Disease, poverty, war and homelessness are not to be ignored. But so much of this unhappiness is man's own doing. Avarice breeds poverty. Fear fathers war. Envy makes for neurosis. Too often we induce our own ailments and project the blame on to blameless people. There is in us a spirit of hostility towards all things. We see creation as cold, people as hostile and God as aloof. People shy from our company and will not listen to our moans. There are moments when we wish we could be free from this confining spirit which keeps us enclosed in a room of resentment. But we may be moved to a brief prayer. "Come, O Holy Spirit." This may be the prelude to release and renewal.

The Spirit of God is the one, true Spirit. And it is the Spirit of Jesus. It is not a wild wind that we can bring under command by whipping up emotions. It is not an intoxicant and does not generate a heady euphoria. It is steady and steadying. It is God active in man. For God is an active God and the human heart the empire of his activity. Only Christ is totally animated by this Spirit and the fruits of the Spirit are the attributes of Christ, the virtues which make a man or woman a transparency of the divine glory. Christ is the locale of the Spirit and to be in Christ is to be naturalised into his mind and emotions. In those who receive the Spirit there is real change; even the glands work differently. There is no other Spirit that is holy. God has no twin. There is only one Son, only one Spirit. To know the Spirit we must turn to Christ and to him only. "The Father and I are one" entails that the Spirit and Christ are one. There are many competing spirits; these are not holy but they are persuasive. They can possess the heart and make it heady. But, how can we detect the true from the false, the holy from the unholy. Only by Christ. The knowledge the Spirit imparts must be consonant with the knowledge of Jesus. The experiences of the Holy Spirit will march with those of Jesus whether in his grief or his glory. We need this power to discriminate. There are many counterfeit spirits abroad and all are seducers.

The present danger is that the cult of the spirit may lead men and women from Christ and become a self-centred exercise, an emotional love-in. This has appeal to hearts made dry by doctrine aridly conveyed and liturgy slovenly performed. The emotions are not to be suppressed; they are true agents of divine experience. But emotions are to be controlled. The artist must work within the limits of his talent and material. The preacher must not preach his own word or invent his own gospel. There is only one Word and one Gospel. The Spirit must not be a reckless experience. It must lead to a deeper knowledge and a more vibrant love of Jesus. The human heart is an open tabernacle and many unworthy spirits seek too occupy it. Jesus is the test. If the Spirit does not glorify him, then some alien energy, some ignoble spirit, is finding admission and there will be no holiness or healing.

It is the Spirit that guarantees every doctrinal formulation. Equally, it is the Spirit alone that authenticates religious experience. Many people see visions and dream dreams. There is no lack of religious experience; there is too much. The visionary is always amongst us. He will claim to have a revelation, even to have seen God and to have received a private communication. But the true Spirit will be known by his closeness to Christ. Not by bizarre manifestations. Christ did not speak in tongues though the Spirit was his only animation. Speaking in tongues is not indispensable to the spiritual person. Love is. Holiness is. But people are attracted by the unusual and esoteric and demand happenings that make headlines. Jesus did not. He said he would send the Spirit. And the Spirit would witness to him. To experience the Spirit is to experience Jesus. And this will show mainly in lives, lived quietly with a strong sense of the centrality of Jesus.

The expense of Spirit

For most of us, religion, like life, is a humdrum thing. We do not lead lives of heroic virtue or spectacular vice. Do we experience the Spirit? We do. But where? Often in temptation. Let us not forget that it was the Spirit that led Christ into the wild and there to be tempted. The Spirit always lives in contention. It does not have an open field but one where there is battle and sometimes defeat. Christ was tempted because he was human. Had he been spared temptation he would not have shared our most harrowing experiences, nor would he have revealed the superiority of the holy. Temptation does not necessarily end in sin and surrender. Most temptations we overcome. But not all. For the Spirit is too weak and the counter-spirit too persuasive. Jesus met temptation and did not succumb. Here we light on the uniqueness of Christ. The Spirit was the flame in him which no contrary force could extinguish. And this Spirit he does not hoard. He releases the Spirit for our health and holiness.

Yet though Jesus in his life in Galilee is possessed by the Spirit, its force is muted and its voice muffled by containment in the flesh. There is a note of conflict when Jesus exclaims "The Spirit is willing but the flesh is weak". Jesus was subject to the weakness that the human condition imposes and he died of weakness, broken and bled white. He gave up the Spirit. Only after his death does the Spirit find freedom from time and place and the fences of human limitation. Only then do we know that the Spirit is not for an élite, an aristocracy of priests and prophets and kings. The Spirit is for all. Pentecost makes the Spirit universal and makes it permanent. It is not an occasional breeze but an enduring influence. It is light for the mind and courage for the heart. It is God active and activating.

The Spirit and the Cross

We experience the Spirit not only on sunny days but when the sky is dark, when we lose our grip on things. It is idle to think that the Spirit will make life all wine and roses. Jesus sees the Spirit as living in contest and the great contest is the agony in Gethsemane. Here the unholy is at its most seductive. Jesus is in his prime and has a following. The prospect of death is too alarming and seems unnecessary. Yet, at another level, he knows that this is the Father's will. And it is the Spirit in him which makes him aware of this paternal request. It is the Father Jesus addresses in that most radical and wrenching of prayers. "Not my will but thine be done." Here is contest, agony, pain. And obedience. And here too is the Spirit as the only light in a dark night, the only leader in a landscape sown with sadness.

The apostles were called to suffer much and the Spirit was the source of their consistency. They carried the cross of Christ because possessed by the Spirit of Christ. Yet the temptation in our time is to divorce the cross and the Spirit. This is to demean both. At Corinth St Paul had to restore sanity to a community where life was all spirit, almost a bacchanalian revel of tongues and marvels and strident prophecy. This was a spirit of a kind. It was not the Holy Spirit for it did not rhyme with the experiences of Christ. So Paul is blunt and deflationary. "We preach

72

Christ crucified." This was a necessary corrective to those who felt the glory of resurrection was at their command. Not so. True, we all want resurrection and its freedom. But there is only one path to resurrection and it is uphill and passes through Calvary. This is sound teaching. There is no theology of the Spirit without a theology of the Cross. This is comforting for those of us whose lives are not marked by miracles and who find each day difficult and made of demand.

Spirit as artist

It is good to cultivate a sensitivity to the Spirit for it is present in the whole chorus of creation. Indeed, the Spirit connects us to creation and confers eyes that see God as artist and as lover. Where there is truth and goodness and beauty, there is the Spirit of God whether in a painting or a person. We cannot live our lives without beauty; it is the signature of God and the seal of his Spirit. A sonnet or a love-song, the face of a girl in her prime, the swoop of a bird, an evening-blue sea or a lonely shore, these are not accidental things but divine poetry composed for our enjoyment. We receive the Spirit that we may become alert. In the Spirit we see through new eyes and can find beauty in every cranny of creation.

The artist cannot paint well unless inspired and the great artists were not merely masters of technique but ministers of a Spirit that impelled them to write and paint and compose. The Suffolk fields and meadows are there for all to see. But Constable sees more and is compelled to reveal the colour and contrasts, the harmony and holiness of a familiar scene yet not visible to unperceiving eyes. L. S. Lowry could find beauty in the industrial waste of the North; human squalor cannot totally erase hidden beauty. There is beauty in the desert.

God is aware that most of us see things through secular eyes. Our disease is dimness. The Spirit confers illumination and each one of us can be an artist. Painting or poetry may be beyond us. But the first art is the art of living. Jesus is the master-artist and his life is his masterpiece. What we call the fruits of the Spirit are simply the virtues of Christ. It is the Spirit eloquent in that precious trio of glorious things, truth, goodness and beauty. Where this holy trinity is absent, the world is a waste-land and people brutalised. But where we see the Spirit active in a man or woman, in a community or consortium, we feel attracted. It is the Spirit that makes Christ attractive. Attraction is the irresistible force and people cannot counter its magnetism. People followed Christ even into the desert. They could not do otherwise.

It is good at times to ponder the artistry of living. Most of us live anonymous lives and there will be nothing to inscribe on our headstone. A name, a date, possibly a text; no more. Yet we should not underrate the gift of being alive. We are little people and God loves little people; that is why he makes so many of us. Fame will not be ours and our name will not be blazoned in lights. No one will write our biography. Yet we are precious people and God did not see fame as the evidence of success. Life lived to the full, love purified, joy relayed, peace imparted, suffering accepted and beauty conveyed; these make the music in the polyphony of living.

It is life that is the gift and the Spirit that gives life enlargement. A great Anglican theologian, a priest, a poet once wrote a sentence that is a challenge to us all. "All may have, if they dare try, a glorious life." This is the voice of George Herbert. But it is also the voice of the Spirit which inspired him in his life and in his art. Notice the little clause — "if they dare try". The Spirit asks for audacity. It is a brisk wind and urges us to live life and not to let it live us. We are failures only if we think we are failures. So many good people think themselves into dejection and their lives are a trudge through a brown corridor lit by a twenty-five watt bulb. They look through wounded eyes on a weary world and their horizon is rimmed by resentment. There the Spirit burns low and there is no beauty in their bearing. Dead people. Only the Spirit can give them life and renovation.

Perhaps the artistry of living consists in a combination of two qualities. Of gentleness and strength. These make for what the world calls "style". It is a good word for each of us has a style and it is all our own. People judge us by our style and the

French wisely identify style with the person. It is not ornament but essence. Not something that can be put on like powder or affected like an accent. We are our style and cannot conceal or cover it. Gentleness without strength softens into sentimentality. Strength on its own makes a bully. But in combination they make for blend and an engaging beauty. Christ was so gentle but never a sequacious character. He was tender to the weak, to women and children and to the casualties of society. But with the rulers he was strong; with oppressors, powerful. The Spirit is both oil and wine. Oil sooths and wine exhilarates. Both are medicines of healing; both mediate holiness. If we have the good fortune to meet a real and rounded personality — and they are rare — we will find them always gentle and always strong. They are artists of living. And of dying. They are people of Spirit.

Spirit as missionary

Christians receive the Spirit that they may enjoy a quality of life for which they were created. Yet, equally, they are called to relay this life for the world's redeeming. Every Christian gift is also a responsibility. All we have, we have received. What we have received, we are called to share. Christianity is not thrift but spend-thrift. Keeping oneself to oneself is not a Christian attitude. This does not mean interference. It does mean concern. Christ does not come for a class or a clique. He comes for all. And those who receive the Spirit are commanded to go, to preach, and to baptise. And to baptise in three names and of one God. In the Father whose service alone allows freedom. In the Son who is now our brother, and holds our hand. In the Spirit who imparts light to the mind and energy to the heart. To be baptised is to be transformed, to be naturalised into Christ, see God as Father, and find fuel in the Spirit. We now have a new name. And to change one's name is to alter one's whole personality. The whole world is different and life has new purpose, new drive, good direction.

This command to go and transform and alert people living hopelessly that something has happened in history, someone has come, is the calling of the Christian. This is commonly known as mission and those who accept this responsibility are known as missionaries. Baptism makes missionaries of us all. It is no easy assignment. Indeed, without the Spirit it is impossible. Peter, who disowned Christ on the night of his arrest appears at Whitsuntide preaching the news of Christ dead and risen. But it was a new Peter, a man transformed and on fire with a received inflammation. He has been converted. And no man or woman can convert. This is the work of the Spirit. The work of the Christian is to water the soil and prepare the soul for reception. Few are naturally receptive to the Spirit. For faith makes demands. It is a gift and a responsibility. It is the obedience that faith demands which provokes our resistance. To believe with the mind is too easy. But faith is a total thing and demands a total change, a total rebirth. Few can take it. Those few who can take it are the salt of the earth. Christians may be a minority but it is minorities who get things done. When Christ died his following was pitifully few. It was enough. The silent majority is a dead weight on the world, a great mass of dough needing yeast for life and enlargement. Salt for meat, yeast for bread, light for the dim, these are Christ's own images for those who receive the Spirit and are commanded to set the world alight.

Yet there is a vast variety of talents through which the Spirit may conduct its fire. Many gifts but one Spirit. Each one of us has a gift, a "charism" to use the Greek word, and every Christian is a charismatic. The Spirit is not relayed through the spectacular but through the ordinary. "Sheer plod makes ploughdown sillion shine" writes the poet. And the common life is plod, daily drag in health and sickness, in wind and weather. What the Spirit teaches is that the real weather is within. This is the last lesson many learn, yet the first schooling in the Spirit. Most work is ninety per cent drudgery. There are few peak moments. But the man or woman of Spirit can find glory merely in perseverance and light in a life of obscurity. Many a flower is born to blush unseen. It still remains a flower and gives glory to God merely by its quiet flowering.

Spirit, then, is to be spent. The message is for mission. The message is simple. It answers a question. The question that ticks and teases everyone of us. "Is a happy life within our reach?" Is history just drift? Am I a failure, a blister on the body of mankind? Is creation futile? How will things end? And how did they begin? Is money really all that matters?

Spirit and the good life

Briefly, can life be good and an experience of glory? The honest heart answers "No". And in the forum of experience, it can make a good case for the prosecution. Disease, earthquake, war, neurosis. The catalogue of crime in the newspapers. Murder and mayhem. Vice and vandalism. So much pain leads man to devise his own analgesic. It is despair. Live without hope; merely endure and die. Accept life as absurd, the world as a warehouse filled with useless things. Look back in anger. And never look forward for there is no future. We all walk a tunnel with no light at its end, and no exit from the impasse. So learn to live with despair.

This grey philosophy can seduce us all. Some sudden bereavement, some betrayal by a friend, some sin or ineluctable sorrow, these assail the heart when most vulnerable. This is the worst temptation and it comes to all. Even to Jesus. And many decent people living in semi-detached houses in quiet suburbs, doing their best for their children and drinking sherry with their neighbours, are, beneath the smiling surface, sad and despairing people. They conceal their sadness. We are surprised when one takes an overdose or asphyxiates himself in his garage. Yet not entirely surprised. We understand. We know.

We know the temptation to see life as meaningless. This is the only question. All others are adjectival. "To be or not to be", that is the question. The Christian answer is an affirmation. But it is not a facile answer. To the blunt question "Is the good life possible?", Christianity answers "No". Unless. Unless something has happened. Unless Someone has happened. Something new. Someone good. We need an event. And the event is a person. Reality is a puzzle written in cipher. We need a word to break the code and Christ is the code-word. He reveals simply what is the case. He is the message and the messenger. It is life we seek and the truth of things. He is the life and he embodies the truth.

For the highest reality is personal and only a person can be the truth. So we look at his life for it is so human, and often so humdrum. Yet his life is all meaning. His responses to people and circumstances are the true responses. His ministry is not just to encourage; it is not to condemn, not even to console. It is to reveal. Reveal the way through the world.

Death, which seems destruction, is revealed as otherwise. This alters our vision of the two great realities — life and death. But more. Jesus remains. The Spirit that saw him through, remains. It is the very breath of Christianity and the Spirit of Christ gives vitality to those who receive its invigoration. The truth remains. And the life is there for all open to its invasion. No one can prove this by logic or argument. Those who receive the Spirit undergo an experience which is the inspiration of their lives. This is their charism and they will relay it through mundane occupations, through work, administration, speech, and actions. With Christ a new and unexpected age has come and the course of history has been mapped. Only with the return of Christ will the drama be completed.

Despair

The Spirit is the corrective to chronic despair. But in the 1980's it is not easy to convey this reality. Pessimism has its attraction. Cynicism exempts us from compassion; we just laugh at the folly of humankind. The plays and novels and films of our time tend to suggest that there is nothing in this world of any value except that which can be bought. The limousine and the gadgetry make the good life. Money, then, becomes the object. And money is necessary and money is good. Good as a servant, but a tyrant if made master. No one ever has enough money. A breathless pursuit of money will make for a life of anxiety.

This is the popular vision and so seductive. But the Spirit teaches other values. Christ used money and saw no virtue in poverty. Poverty is a sin which the poor do not commit. But there is another and deeper poverty and this is the deprived and desponding heart. Money cannot fill its coffers and gadgets cannot give it love. Love is not a human artefact but a gift of the Spirit and it is the great donation. The world is half-aware of this. The spiritual are totally aware. That is the secret of their calm, of their confidence, of their peace and power. Sorrow comes. It saddens but does not destroy. Disappointments occur and they wound but do not kill. Death comes but it is not extinction but the last avenue to completeness.

Spirit as prayer

The Christian, then, is called to convey the news of Christ. He cannot do it alone. The Spirit must give him knowledge and courage. And in Christians the Spirit can burn low. Devotions can become mechanical, liturgy can be lifeless, prayer perfunctory and preaching arid. The salt, Jesus warns, can lose its savour. How he dreads the smooth pride of the merely pious. When the Spirit is a flickering flame there is no re-kindling without a resort to prayer. It is so trite to talk of prayer, almost too easy to offer it as a panacea. No presumption is worse than to accept that we know what prayer is or that we know how to pray. Prayer is not a natural exercise. "Lord, teach us to pray" asked the apostles. The answer was brief. Say "Our Father". And, of course, we cannot. God is so exalted, we such underlings. Only a son or daughter can say "Our Father". Only in Christ can we pray. We need a new confidence to be able to address God not as "Your Majesty" but simply, intimately, endearingly as "Abba, Father". This confidence is not easy to the heart. Only the Spirit can make the heart bold and lead it to utter that fine and filial address. Almost the whole of Christianity is condensed in those words "Abba, Father".

Then what do we say next? We do not know. Better to say nothing and let the Spirit slowly begin to be our spokesman for the Spirit is deep within us, the breath within our lungs. We must accept what is hard to accept — that the Spirit knows our needs better than we do. So it is wise to become a wind-instrument, empty of all sound and impediment, and just let the heart receive the music when it comes. Then the Spirit teaches us strange and wonderful things about our own interior confusion. He orders our emotions and overcomes our dissipation. We may begin prayer feeling ragged and resentful. The Spirit gives us wisdom to know what we could not know by self-analysis or introspection. We emerge with a new consciousness, a true consciousness. It is a hard but healthy exercise. There is no substitute for prayer. Good works, philanthropy, committees have their place. But they cannot stand in for prayer and make it an extra. The person of Spirit is a person of prayer. This is an exact equation. Christ prayed to the Father. But through the Spirit. We never pray alone. Neither did Jesus.

I BELIEVE IN THE HOLY, CATHOLIC CHURCH

The Spirit of God needs a hearth and a home. If it is not to be a random breeze, a reckless energy. It must be earthed in time and in place. And in people. It must be seen. Like the spire of a village church, a mile from the motorway, it must arrest the eye and point. Point where? To the sky and the great spaces which speak of realities, sacred and sublime, far beyond our reach yet not beyond our desire.

The Church is not a human consortium, a religious multinational, nor primarily a structure, not first an institution. The Church has an institution. But it is not an institution. Christ is the Church's one foundation. Peter, James and John are not founders of the Church. They are churched by the Church. There is no word of comparison for the Church, no synonym. It is antecedent to its members. St Paul lends his genius to try and convey the uniqueness of the Church. He employs two metaphors. To suggest its closeness to Christ he calls the Church his body. To denote its difference he calls the Church his bride. But even Paul cannot find an image equal to the reality. The Church always carries the flavour of mystery. We can understand in part; we cannot exhaust. As we grow in faith the mystery becomes more meaningful and the light less opaque. But we must let the Church keep its secret.

The Church stands on an event. One event. The event can be put only in a hyphenated word: death-resurrection. This event is decisive. It alters all things. Had Christ not died he would not have been one of us. Death takes us all. Had Christ not risen ours would be a sorry condition; life would be heavy and hope-

81

F

less, its terminus extinction. There would be nothing to live for, nothing to die for. But our hope rises with the rising of Christ and our tired hearts find relief from the oppression of too many sorrows.

Yet because Christ died there is danger of seeing him held by the past like some outsize hero. But a dead Christ cannot help or heal us. The Christ we need is a Christ active, alive and full of energy. The infant Church was composed of people not dressed in the black of mourning, not chanting sad odes or elegies, but people alive and intoxicated with the wine of an event. Three words sing their joy. "Christ is risen." Not Christ has risen. Christ is alive, is here, is present through the Spirit; dead hearts are bold and bright again. The Spirit which was Christ's only energy is now the force and fire of common people. They are no longer dead and despondent; they are different. They have undergone that transforming experience we call "conversion". Once cowards, now they have courage. Once dejected, now they are lit with hope. One dead, now they are alive.

The twice-born

The Church is composed of the re-born. This is the work of the Spirit. They are gifted people, other Christs. For the gifts of the Spirit are the engaging virtues of Christ and attract even the jaundiced eye. They love wildly, carelessly, totally. They are free, released from all those deadening things that make us shy from people an dshrink from God. They are not sinless. But sin no longer holds the centre of their consciousness. Aware of sin, they are more aware of the love and liberality of God. They believe, they hope, they love. And they live. It is life that is the one force of attraction on this planet. For where we see a person gloriously alive we see God and his Spirit kindling this cold earth. The Church is called to evidence that life is the stronger force. For many this is hard to believe. They need a sign. They seek a sign. And only a community of people clearly alive, doing battle with disease and death, contending with despair, can convince and convert each faltering heart.

82

What, then, is the first work of the Church? It is to make present the great event. And the event is a person. A person who lived, died and was raised. Raised above history and beyond the frontier of time and place. He is in history; and he is over history. He needs a home and his home is the Church, a community of people, different in so many things, but one in their allegiance to their Lord. One Lord, one faith, one baptism; this trilogy is the ground of cohesion which human acrimony will never subvert. The Church then has no meaning without Christ; it has no power without his Spirit. It has no function save, in the most real sense, to re-present the event and the person until time is no more and the long travail ended.

To honour its function of re-presentation, the Church needs an institution. It needs bishops and priests and deacons. It needs law and regulation. It needs preachers and administrators. Yet these have no autonomous function. They are at the service of the event, the person and the revelation. Because the Church is composed of men and women, tempted to worship at the altar of ambition, the Church will often be a flickering lamp. When faith is strong the re-presentation will be vivid, passionate and appealing. It will have beauty and aptness and the quiet melody of the holy. There will be saints; there will be mystics. The Spirit will warm like gentle fire and the presence of God will be perceived like the perfume of a rose in Summer bloom. There will be small emphasis on law. There will be the felt magnetism of love. There will be poets and artists and preaching of quality. For the Church is an author of art and an agent of beauty. Fine art can be a revelation of holy and hidden things. It can impart to secular eyes the beauty of the sacred and the glory of the sublime.

When faith is weak and watery the re-presentation will continue. Though the Spirit can be quelled it cannot be quenched. But liturgy will be mechanical, preaching arid, prayer a tedium. The Church will not be creative and will not speak the Good News with the eloquence of conviction. The accent will rest on law and obligation. There will be a return to casuistry and legal nicety. And the world will declare the Church dead, a precious relic of past glory, but no longer healing, no longer helpful. And there will be contention in the Church. The sad will want to return to the past and opt out of present history. Others will be eager to reform the style of the Church, its liturgy and language; to make new approaches, to create more supple structures.

The Church — a sign and sacrament

Some may despair of the Church and see the institution as blockage, as total impediment. This is a danger. For the institution is necessary. True, it may overrate its role and arrogate to itself powers it does not possess. It may fail to see itself as the acolyte of the event, the person and the revelation. Stressing its authority, it may become authoritarian. It may dominate where it should serve. It may silence when it should listen. It may condemn when it should forgive. These are the temptations that come to all in power. History teaches that power, not money, is the author of corruption. Spiritual power is the most potent of all. Yet the Church needs an institution as the body needs a skeleton, for order and articulation. An invertebrate Church would be a corpse.

The Church must point. Like a village steeple it must lead the eye away from itself to the heights of the holy. If the Church does not point, it will disappoint. The world will say it is pointless and they will look to secular shrines at which to worship. The temptation of the institution is to see itself as all-sufficient, as an autonomous empire, a closed kingdom. Then it will no longer be a sign. It will point only to itself and seek glory in that unholy trinity of power, prestige and possessions. It will not concern itself with preaching but with self-preservation. It will not see itself as ministry but as mastery. Jesus was well aware of this seduction, aware that the salt might lose its savour, that the light might be hid under a bushel or a bureaucracy.

Yet the Church has endless powers of recovery for the Spirit, though not its exclusive possession, will always remain to rekindle its dying embers. Indeed, the history of the Church is so often a history of a decline that did not become a dissolution. Some prophetic voice speaks and no one can silence its anger. Catherine of Siena reproves the Pope. Francis of Assisi reproves

84

the gold and glamour of the prelates. The Spirit often speaks through unimportant people. The institution can never suffocate the voice of prophecy.

The point of the Church

The Church must point. To its Lord. It must be a sign, a sacrament. If the Church does not point to its Lord it is insignificant. It will appear as a business, over-organised and absorbed in its own internal mechanics. Sacrament is the key to understanding the Church. Sacrament is a sign that achieves what it signifies. A hand-shake seals reconciliation. It is sign. But it does something. Indeed, life is lived by signs and a smile or a greeting can restore drooping spirits. Love has no language, except that of signs and without the signs love evaporates and expires. Christ lamented his followers' inability to read the signs of the times and sought to cure this illiteracy. He did not point to himself. He pointed to his Father and saw himself as the sacrament of the Father. "He who sees me sees the Father" asks for a sacramental imagination.

The Church is not for the Church. The Church is for the world. It is not to rule the world; a theocracy is invariably hard and oppressive. The world has a right to be the world and to seek its own betterment by its own endeavours. But the world is wounded and aware that it is not what it should be. So many wars lead men to conclude that the world is a lost place and that there is no remedy that is radical, no hope of real redemption. Christ does not deny that the evil in the world is massive. He asserts he has overcome the world and its brutality. But is this true? We look for a sign, for a new light in a dismal sky.

It is idle to claim that church-people are better than those with no religious affiliation. Folly to assert that believers are better than unbelievers. Indeed, it is impossible to assess one's own faith, to know if one believes or merely believes one believes. St Augustine has a cautionary remark. "God has many the Church does not have; the Church has many God does not have." The habit does not make the monk and baptism may end in barren-

85

ness. The person who says "I have the faith, thank God" may be guilty of a deception. We cannot be monitors of our emotions.

The Church is not opposed to the world. Indeed, the Church is the world realised and made conscious of its true character. The Church is called to be the sign that God is deep in the world, its centre of gravity. He is a magnet attracting men to be brothers not by looking at each other but by looking towards him. The Church judges the world's restlessness. It is restless because it seeks to be at peace, aches to be at peace, but has not the means. Christ reveals that God is no spectator. He is a participant. He wants to save not to condemn. He sends his Son. And the Church is ordained to this same redeeming work. It is the world's servant, the world's light and lover.

The temptations of the Church

At present the institutional Church is undergoing reform. It must always undergo reform. For it is eternally tempted to see itself as the end. Yet it is only the means to the end; it is the instrument not the music. Its authority is real but derived, and it must not pretend to a knowledge or a power greater than that of its Lord. It must see authority as Christ sees it; as the only author of freedom. Its work is to further the growth of true personalities, living not in dread, but rather as flowers that grow under the sun and in the daylight. A religion of fear is a religion of falsehood. It will not attract because it is not attractive. It will not be a sign but a counter-sign. People will simply leave. For people need freedom as they need food. To be themselves.

In writing about the Church one is conscious of a certain un-reality, of describing a Church that never was. The strongest argument against the Church is its history. Few quarrel with its ideals; many question its performance. Hypocrisy is the charge. It is best not to deny it but to admit it. For the Christian is aware that he falls short and will always fall short. Hypocrisy is lethal only when denied. Christ calls on the people in power to look behind the facade and confront the falsehood that lies concealed like a cancer. It is easy to say "Lord, Lord". Profession is always easy. "Their lips are with me." But the truth has its tabernacle in the heart. And "their hearts are far from me". A wedge can be driven between what we say and what we are. This is hypocrisy and there is no greater sadness, no more subtle sin. But that sin can be forgiven. Christ employs language of invective to those in power. Yet only to save them. Hypocrisy cannot survive the light; it breeds in the dark. He uncovers hypocrisy in order to release people from its grip. Kindness would congeal. Shock brings release.

Conversion and consciousness

Consciousness is the key. Man on his own does not know who he is, what he is for, why he is here. Nor does the world. The Christian is a person conscious of his identity, knowing his purpose, set on a road. His consciousness marches with that of Christ. Every Christian is a convert. And conversion finds its focus in a new awareness. The convert believes that this world is still a good world, well worth redeeming. The Church should show the world what it can be, what it wants to be, what it will be. This may seem like bland optimism. And Christianity is an optimist. The Church betrays its calling when its language is fixated on sin and is always sad and sighing. "Take courage: I have overcome the world" should be the slogan of the Christian.

The Church proclaims the news that God is present in the world to bring it to its completion. It does not deny the reality of death. It preaches Christ crucified. And risen. And it does not merely preach. It celebrates. It celebrates a death; this death. For Calvary alone discloses the malevolence of death. It kills God. Sin has its hour on Calvary. It is easy for the world to believe in Calvary; there is so much death. Death darkens every horizon. It is resurrection that for ever alters the consciousness of the Christian. Here the power of the good, the reality of grace, the energy of the Spirit declare themselves. And in this our world. To interiorise these truths is to be transformed. Only a new consciousness can transform a man or woman, can release and liberate them from a life of diffused misery and endless moan. The Church preaches Good News. But hearing is not enough.

People want to sing and the Church is best seen as the Church when it celebrates and sings its psalms and songs.

The meal

The classic symbol of celebration is the meal. And there is more to the meal than meets the eye. So rich is its symbolism that it is hard to enumerate its aspects. It affirms need. Need for food, need for affection. A person invited to supper may not be short of food. He may be short of friendship. And the meal may be an agent of transformation. For here the shy become articulate, the cynic softens his asperities, the lonely find they are loved. It was around a table that Christ did much of his redeeming work and the bread and wine were more than common food, but signs, effective signs, of his care for all who were willing to come and eat. His parting words were spoken at supper. And here he gave more than bread and wine but himself and totally. Through the genius of sacrament he gave and he gives what all men seek — life and a larger life. The price was high. A death, no less. But death freely given is sacralised and love speaks most eloquently through sacrifice. "Greater love than this, no man has." It is sacrifice that subverts sin. And love without sacrifice lacks steel and stamina. We celebrate a death for it is the sacrifice that redeems all who come and freely admit their need. Their need for a love not native to the human heart, for a food rich in the protein of affection.

The Church is not a humanitarian organisation. Its primary work is not social. Its first work is worship and worship is worthship. It orders priorities and reveals what alone is of supreme worth. It worships God. As Christ is the sign and sacrament of the Father, the Church is the sign and sacrament of Christ. It may do many other works and serve good causes. Yet these are secondary. The world can heal many of its own wounds by charitable exercises. Only the Church can preach and proclaim the presence of God in this bleeding world. It does this by word and by sacrament. The word it preaches is not its own word. Nor is the preacher his own man with his own gospel. He can preach only a given gospel. This is the gospel of the Lord. And every gospel is one of redemption.

The movement of the Mass

The Mass begins realistically; where we are. We are out of true, at odds with ourselves, with people and with God. So we say "Lord, we have sinned against you". This is a terrible saying. Yet true. We ask for mercy and there is absolution. The readings make Christ present by their proclamation of his work of rescue. Every gospel is a difficult gospel for our thoughts are not God's thoughts and too easily we superimpose a human interpretation. So we need the homily to reveal the hidden and healing content. Then we are encouraged to offer ourselves to God through the bread and wine and move towards communion. We naturally shy from communion. The holiness of God is a deterrent; our sin makes us shy. We feel unworthy. But the Church does not ask for worthiness. Only for willingness. How consoling that the last word before communion is "Lord, I am not worthy". We receive the real Christ in order to build up the body of the world. But, first, the community must be made one. Consisting of sinners, it is dismembered. In the Eucharist we are re-membered. Re-membered, with Christ and with one another. His sacrifice was not in vain and the Mass mediates its fruit and its fire. We are re-membered. And our consciousness finds composure in peace. The Mass ends with a kind of command. "Go." Go where? To the world. And how? In peace. We are at peace with ourselves, with people. And with God. And the world wants peace and seeks peace as a bird seeks the air. The peace it seeks it cannot generate by political agreements. It means a deeper peace; the Church is commanded to relay it. To go in peace.

A Church of sinners

It is not difficult for many people to say with conviction "I believe in God". Nor is it difficult to see in Christ his unique self-disclosure. But to believe in the Church, there lies the rub. So much contention, so much avarice, so much harshness, so much sin. Yet the Church is for the sinner. Which means that the Church is for all. A Church composed of saints would be no use to us. Who would dare ask for admission to that elite? The saint is merely a sinner who has died and been fully reborn. A hypocrite who has admitted his hypocrisy and seen the light. A weak and wayward person, blown by various winds, who has been caught by the Spirit of God and given direction.

All need direction. Left to ourselves we cannot find the way. Left to ourselves we have weak motivation. The Church is given for our direction. It is fashionable to say that religion cannot be taught, only be caught. This is mistaken. There must be teaching, given truths that disclose the origin and end of human existence. The Church must be a teaching Church and a preaching Church. The great truths cannot be caught by unaided imagination. Left to himself, man will mould a god in his own too human image. And the god man makes of his own imagining is a tyrant. A god of revenge or a god who is remote, a sky-god, living on self-admiration.

So the Church must have a creed. Emotion is not enough. There must be fact and these facts must be cased in propositions. The proposition will never fully articulate the fact; language is too rigid and words too brittle. But the proposition is necessary. It is pointer to the truth which it contains but can never exhaust. "I believe in God" is a proposition. But it says more than it seems to say. It declares that I cannot live my life on my own resources.

Religion — taught and caught

Humility begins here. It declares that the human mind, the most able, the most agile, cannot discover the rhythms of reality. It asserts that I cannot live on what I know. Knowledge leaves us living in the red. "Science", said one great scientist, "tells us nothing important." The great truths are received truths and it is not the mind that receives them, but the mind, the heart and the hand. "I believe in God" is not assent of the mind but a total submission. The mind is enlightened, the heart moved, the hand given energy. A new person is born and he regards all things differently. People and circumstances, life and death, God and people. This new person is blest with a new consciousness. He or she lives by faith. This faith must be taught. The Church must be a teacher. Faith must be taught.

Religion must also be caught. It must engage the feelings. For the feelings give access to reality and we live largely by our emotions. The Church must have feel, have fragrance, must vibrate. Above all, the Church must attract. And there is only one enduring source of attraction on this wounded planet. We call it love, or truth, or the good. Here we pass beyond mere knowledge and move into the foot-hills of mystery. "I believe in God" begins to glow and hum. The heart is touched and breaks from the iron cage of self-absorption. Something dies; it is that timid attachment to the self which lives behind defences and is afraid of God and people. "I believe that" becomes "I believe in". The "taught" becomes the "caught" and there is a new birth and a felt belief.

To enter the Church is to die. Let us not underrate this hard surrender. It is no easy exercise. It is a descent into the water from which we cannot emerge by our own endeavour. The child is raised from the font by a given energy, by a Spirit not its own. Now it is no longer condemned to be its own leader or to live by its own illumination. It has the Father for its security; the Spirit for its maturity. It is naturalised into Christ and must learn to see with his eyes, and to feel with his heart. For this it needs help and that help is mediated through the community we call the Church. Grace is given to the body of believers; it is in the body we find security and salvation.

The neighbour

This truth is not to everyone's taste. Many would prefer a one-to-one relationship with God and to dispense with any go-between. Some instinct wants to love God and to ignore the neighbour. The tower of Babel is the first symbol of this deep desire; God by direct climb. It lingers in us all. The early Church saw many men going into the desert to seek perfection in lonely places. St Gregory was disturbed. 'If you go into the desert", he wrote, "whose feet will you wash?" A telling point. He sees the recluse as rejecting the stern command to love God and people with the same love. He sees the Church as not for me but for all. St John is not given to strong language but he does pen one abrasive sentence. He declares that the man who says he loves God and loves not his neighbour is, simply, a liar. He may be unaware of the lie. The Church must be his accuser.

The neighbour is the test; the neighbourhood is our parish. Jesus was no recluse and his life was not lived in a cloister. His love for the Father entailed a love of us all. He called all people to the meal, yet most declined his invitation. For the meal makes a demand, the demand to share our company with other people. The world seeks to be one but people are naturally sectarian. The Church is not to be a coterie of the like-minded; then it would be a source of divide. It is called to be catholic, and, in a sense, chaotic. Not virtue or moral excellence or a good education make the condition of entry. Faith suffices. And faith fruits and flowers in love, a love which is impartial and, to the godless heart, impossible. With God all things are possible. Even love of the neighbour. This is the strangest revelation of all and the Church must be its witness.

It will witness the presence of God active and animating the world in a variety of ways. Through works of mercy and channels of charity. A frightening chapter in the gospel of St Matthew acts a drama of the last assize. And, when the crunch comes, there is only one question. I was hungry; did you give me to eat? It is the pronoun "me" that surprises. Christ is not a holy picture but incarnate in the little and lonely people of this world. To be a member of the Church is a privilege; but a privilege which carries a responsibility. We are responsible for those in need and that includes all mankind. To accept this responsibility asks for a heart of sympathy. We are not naturally sensitive to those in need for many are wastrels. No matter; we are called to be indiscriminate, to have tenderness for the undeserving. Jesus entered the house of Zacchaeus; there was no greater oppressor of the poor. That visit was the means of his conversion. Christ has sharp eyes and saw in this exploiter a good man but overlaid by avarice. He released the Christ-man within him. He loved the neighbour. He alone.

The primary work of the Church

Yet works of mercy are not the first works of the Church. The first work resides in its liturgy. We must receive before we can give. We must commune before we can communicate. We must worship so that God will occupy the centre of our consciousness and be the octane of inspiration. The pressures of work and daily worries persuade us to seek salvation in secular things and to worship at the altar of the wage. The first sin is idolatry. Work is the contemporary idolatry and the wage its sacrament. Liturgy releases us from idolatry; that is its function. It orders. It re-orientates. It does not speak human thoughts but the thinking of God. And this is our salvation from common sorrows. During six days of the week the weight of things can press too hard and take us from the holy. We become nervy, depressed and afraid. Our faith falters, our spirit loses its spark. We come to the altar not first to receive but to give. To give ourselves back to God, to offer our sorrows and sins and ourselves with a kind of child-like helplessness. We are answering the kind call of Jesus; come to me all you who labour and are burdened. Offertory must precede communion. Merely to go to church, no matter how false or faithless we feel, is an action of great worth. It is faith seeking greater faith. It is the priest and people's high responsibility to see that the liturgy is wonderfully alive, that it relays the fire and forgiveness of God. Truth speaks through beauty, through the right employment of words and music and gesture. The liturgy must have feel. It must relay the presence of the holy in every detail of the rite, in every rubric. For here is the primary sign of the real presence of Christ earthed among us and eager to restore our trembling spirits. A dead liturgy, a rushed Mass, will not be a sign, but a counter-sign. People will simply go away. They came for bread; they were given a stone.

The Church may wonder why it no longer attracts and there is no easy answer. But where the eucharist is seen as central and worship given primacy there is no need to fear. New structures, new devotions, new theology will make a contribution. But worship in spirit and truth will always win. The holy has a unique authority over the mind and the emotions and the desire for the holy is endemic in mankind. In the East the holy man has a place in society which people recognise as necessary. He does nothing in particular; he prays. In the West he would be considered a parasite; for he does not work. But in the East he is a sign of the primacy of God and the need for worship. People accord him veneration and supply. In his person and his poverty he incarnates the holy.

The holy

Holiness cannot be defined. "Holy, Holy, Holy" is the angels' mysterious address to God. Only God can receive the adjective "holy"; other applications are analogous. Holiness cannot be defined. It can be recognised. We see it, first, as power which is more than a human attribute. The holy person is equal to circumstance, no matter how hostile, to pain no matter how piercing, and to death, his own or those whom he loves. Holiness is harmony; head and heart and hand work as one and there is no interior dislocation. Their lips are with God; so are their hearts.

The holy person is a person possessed. Some divine influence is the force which imparts peace to this personality. Most of us are too anxious and we accept anxiety as we accept colds or headaches, as inevitable trials of living. Christ's "be not anxious" seems like pious idealism, desirable but impossible. Yet anxiety is not invincible; that is the history of the saints. Fret, wobble, touchiness are symptoms of a deep malaise and are not to be accepted as mere irritants. The Church does not take anxiety lightly and, as the mass moves towards communion, it prays a good prayer. "Keep us free from sin and protect us from all anxiety."

For anxiety is the pre-condition of sin. Were we not anxious we would not be envious, not slander, not indulge in self-pity, not see the world as a damned and destitute place. Where there is deep anxiety there is distrust. Distrust of God. Either he is incompetent; and cannot help. Or he is indifferent; and will not help. It is indifference that most deters. It is self-induced numbness to protect ourselves against the pain of the world. The Church must be the sign and sacrament of Christ. And Christ reveals that God cares. If the Church seems indifferent to the sorrows of mankind and merely warns or condemns, then it will betray its mission. Its mission is to save. From beginning to end the liturgy is strong with this urge to return to man and woman their faith in God and in themselves. "Your sins are forgiven; your faith has made you whole." This is the refrain in every liturgy but the music must be heard and the truth told to the heart in need of healing. It is the heart Christ seeks to possess and rectify. For the worst break is heart-break. Only God can mend this dislocation.

Holiness is wholeness. At Mass we commune with the holy. Yet we may shy from this intimate approach. We need company; we need encouragement. Sin isolates. Its viciousness resides in separation, in a life with God and at odds with people. It is a lonely thing; not living but partly living. To be is to belong. The Church is the community which will accept anyone who believes that God believes in him. Without Jesus we could hardly accept that God believes in us, indeed admires us. Loves us. Without the Church we could not realise that belief, activate it, make communion true, make peace palpable. We would have religion in the head. That is no use. Religion must be total. Religion must be personal and passionate. And when we see a real Christian we are aware we are in the presence of a power not merely human. We feel the flavour of the holy, the nearness of God.

Beauty

The holy has beauty. Beauty is not addition. Beauty is essence. The Church which is the mother of sanctity is also the mother of art. All great art is praise. And to praise is good. We praise what we appraise, what we appreciate. The Church must reveal the praiseworthy, what is good and true and sublime. The heart can be seduced to praise unworthy things and to idolise unworthy people. The mob opted for Barabbas and sneered at Christ. The Church is called not only to reveal what is true and what is false. Not only what is good and what is evil. But, not least, what is beautiful and what is repellent. Art is the author of beauty and the great artist praises God in his creations. The world could survive if it ran out of oil. But the oil-painting would remain. For the artist has vision and sees in a face or a field the beauty of God and a little of his wonder. Art, poetry and religion go into decline simultaneously. For each is inspired by the same Spirit. And the Spirit may burn low, the vision of God be dimmed, the light of the world occluded. Then art will become tawdy, poetry obscure, and religion anaemic.

The contemporary Church is looking to its structures and organisation. This is necessary work, yet not primary. Efficiency is not the first virtue. It is the virtue of organisation. And the Church is not an organisation but a people seeking to be one and holy by communion with the One and Holy. So it is good to see that the Church must be more than efficient. It must be effective as a sacrament is effective by imparting the life and love of God to dejected hearts. Where the emphasis is on law and exactness there is danger that the Spirit may be silenced under the weight of reports and resolutions.

The administrator

The administrator has a key place in the Church. He provides order and order is a pre-condition of freedom. There must be law; there must be regulation. The danger is that law and regulation may become primary and love die of malnutrition. St Paul becomes shrill in his admonitions about the danger of law seeking to subdue the Spirit. And he knew what he was talking about for he had lived under a law that almost broke his great heart. Yet he was no anarchist. The law has its value. It kills. Kills out sense of competence. For we cannot keep the law. Here we reach impasse. St Paul gives exit. "But the Spirit gives life." And it is life we seek. And the glory of life is the wind of freedom.

The administrator makes for order. Who makes for freedom?
The prophet. Prophet and administrator make the poetry and
prose of the Church, the music and words of its motet. Prophets
are rare people. They disturb. Their language is inflammatory,
their words violent, their message "Listen". The prophet is deep
in history and in love with the original revelation. He has rare
insight, deep inspiration. He laments any perversion of the original
utterance and is critical of the present. He wishes to conserve the
true and is dismayed by the accretions that time and self-interest
have imposed on the pure and given endowment. So he is opposed.
He dies violently or in exile. The grave is his pulpit.

Jesus loved the prophets with a rare affection. He lamented
that they went unheard, that the voice of God was silenced and
the prophet dishonoured mainly by those he had come to save.
Yet this is human. There is seduction in the status quo, something
cosy and comforting in the familiar. Christ knew the pain of the
prophet and was opposed by those who corrupted the law to
serve their ambition. By and large, it was the powerful, the priests
and prelates, who had made service into privilege and already
received their reward. It was the common people who followed
Christ and who listened attentively for here they heard not a party
or political broadcast but the truth. The truth carries its own
authority. People recognise it as of God for it passes the only test
of truth. It makes free. It releases the heart from the burden of
false obligations. It allays scrupulosity. It sedates anxiety. It makes
people unafraid and they come to God speaking, singing, "Father,
we come to you with praise and thanksgiving".

The Church always has its prophets. Usually they are opposed. Cardinal Newman was a man of prophecy. Deep in the
scriptures, a patristic scholar, he could read the signs of his own
century and predict the course of ours. He found little support
from authority, but was not deterred. The prophet has courage.
He knows the truth always has a hard passage; people prefer the
easy and expedient. But the insights of Newman lent fire to the
Second Vatican Council. For this Council too was prophetic and
sought to recover the original revelation and present it in the

accent and idiom of our own time. So the Council disturbed and met resistance. But the Spirit can be quelled but never quenched and the seed has already found sufficient soil. The harvest will come and it will be abundant.

Freedom is how the truth is apprehended by the heart. Only God is totally free. Human freedom is "freedom under". Under God. "Call no man your Father" writes the charter of Christian freedom. "You have one Father who is in heaven." That is, he transcends all human paternities. If God is dethroned then some man becomes god. And he is a monster. Atheist countries are rarely benign. The party or the dictator is man usurping divinity. It is for the Church to reveal that freedom and order are not incompatible. Christ was obedient to the Father. Yet what he did, he did freely. It was the obedience of a son, deeply in love. It was the freedom of a son, deeply loved. And it is to sonship not to servitude that Christ calls everyone. The Church must witness in everything it does, in everything it says, that man is born to be free to be his true self and only God is Father. It is this freedom that all seek and few find. For there is a fear of freedom as there is a fear of God. Jesus says "Fear not". The Church must be unafraid. Then it will need few rules and no rhetoric. It will quite convincingly use that lovely phrase "the freedom of the children of God". And it will attract a world now grown nervous and too afraid.

THE COMMUNION OF SAINTS

The word "saint" is off-putting to the half-and-half Christian. It suggests either harshness or heroism, a sanctity that soars too high beyond the friendly foot-hills. We are so conscious of our faults, so pained by our defections, to look on the heights which the saint inhabits. We admire saints and, when young, may be urged to imitate them, sometimes wisely, sometimes not. The young priest, St John Vianney, lived on rotting potatoes when first ordained. Grown older he remarked "Only a foolish young man would have done that". Holiness is not the inhuman. Holiness is the human at its best.

Such a pity that the word "saint" has been haloed and saintliness seen as eccentric. The saint is concentric. The original meaning of saint is just "baptised". St Paul addresses his converts as saints but no man was more critical of their failings. A saint is a sinner who has been converted. This takes time; a lifetime. Curiously as they grow in sanctity, they become more conscious, not less, of their sin. And this does not depress them. Rather, it makes them more forceful through the energy in that fire we call "grace". Grace must overcome something. It must repair the flaws in our human nature. "Grace has conquered nature; that is the history of the saints". So wrote Newman. From experience.

To understand the communion of saints we need a picture. Baptism supplies one. A child, parents, godparents; these make a miniature community, the whole Church in microcosm. The child is naturalised into that community all of them baptised. By birth the child belongs to a natural family of parents, brothers and sisters. By grace it is naturalised into a community both larger and more enlarging. Its natural family will diminish and die. There will be death and bereavement. There will be loneliness. The need for good company will remain; the need for com-

99

munion become more acute. One may try to disown this need and seek isolation and opting out. Yet this is not the sane way. Not the way of life and increase. No one is an island; no one an isolate.

The baptised are called to communion; that is their vocation. Baptism does not end at the font; it begins there. Baptism is not fulfilment. It is promise. It is a seedling and needs nutrition if it is to grow and germinate. Notice how many of Christ's metaphors speak of rich soil and good husbandry. Baptism is for growth. As the child is baptised no one can predict whether its promise will find fulfilment or stay sterile as a stone. So much depends on those people standing shyly around. They are asked to give the child protection and another parentage. They compose a communion, a communion of saints and the future of this saintling is committed to their keeping.

Yet, is this asking too much of common people? It is. For parents and godparents are not angels. They too are sinners and in daily need of a diet more sustaining than their own endeavours. The Eucharist supplies this need and makes possible the fulfilment of their baptismal promise. Baptism is not for baptism; it is for Eucharist. And only in Eucharist do we experience real and realised communion. In the quiet of an evening chapel, men and women and children move towards the altar to receive. To receive communion. For we cannot make communion no matter how extrovert or gregarious. We do not make one body by looking at each other. Only by looking in the same direction and being embodied in the one body of the one Lord. Unity is not native to man; discord is the loudest music. Unity is the glory of God. Man can only receive it. Only then does he experience what his heart prays and pines for. Communion with God and with people. This is the peace the world can never give.

To be or to belong

Yet we do not receive communion merely for personal satisfaction. We receive to give. The Mass ends not with congratulation but with a command. "Go". The peace we have received we are called to impart. To whom? To anyone. We receive the real body of Christ to build the body of mankind. For the world aches for peace. And despairs of it. It sees this place as a desert, dead and dry with no spring of fresh and flowing water. Each day some die of starvation, others of excess. This great, big world is a field sown with envy. The only peace is the pseudo-peace of oppression.

Yet the world looks, searches, hopes. The best known commendation accorded to the first Christians was simple. "See how these Christians love each other." Rare tribute. And now quoted in irony. A divided Christianity is the worst scandal. It suggests a divided God. Yet God has no favourites and holds all in his sympathy and invites all to his supper. Nor does he ask for worthiness. Only for willingness. Willingness to believe, in communion, real communion with God and peace with mankind. A dream? A dream indeed but the best achievements begin as a dream in the heart which believes in the impossible.

"Lord, I am not worthy" is the admission of the sinner. "Only say the word and I shall be healed." This is the slogan of the saint. The communion of saints is born of the holy things given in the Eucharist. God alone is holy. Man is born unholy, yet with a reach for holiness, an urge to commune with something, someone larger than himself. Loneliness is littleness. It is living in an attic, too small, too airless. We need to belong to something larger than our secluded self. So astronomers study the stars, explorers walk the ice of the Antarctic, the sailor communes with the ocean. And everyone seeks the affection of family and friends. To be is to belong.

Gathered by God

Holiness is not a condition of entry into the Church. But the desire for holiness is. The really holy person is unaware of his holiness. He is only aware of the holiness of God. At first this makes him afraid. Indeed, fear is the first grace. Yet it is not terror. It is awe. It is the fear that silences and subdues when we watch the night-sky and its riot of stars and are aware of our own unimportance. It is a fear which attracts as the peak of Everest both intimidates and attracts the climber. It is Christ who makes God no longer fearful but fatherly. The sheer holiness of God would be a dissuasive did we not see him at home in common, human clay. In Christ we see God no longer as fear but as fatherly. The communion of saints is no human consortium, no club or confederacy. Its cohesion does not derive from its members. It is the family of those gathered by God not by good will. Such people are animated by a Spirit more than philanthropy. They are people inspired and strong with a strength which is more than bravado. They are powerful because possessed. So the child is baptised in three names and is accorded fellowship with Father, Son and Spirit. This is no minor induction. It is radical. It is rebirth. And it continues. Death is the last baptism and heaven is communion fully and finally realised.

There are many saints among us and they walk the world incognito. Canonisation is for the few; communion for all. As November opens, the Church celebrates saints unknown to us but known to God. They may be parents or friends. All were born sinners yet did not allow sin to be overlord. Alone, they were helpless. But the Church has an open door, and like a mother with generous arms calls all the sick, all the sinful. They are saved, but not by themselves. They find salvation in that community where bread and wine are consecrated for all.

THE FORGIVENESS OF SINS

Christianity turns on a single word. The word is "forgiveness". Do not think you understand it. Do not even think you believe it. Those who believe in the forgiveness of sins are rare people, the salt of the earth. Not that they are sinless. Not at all. Only that they believe that the love of God is fire; it consumes their sin and liberates them from the entail of guilt. The people most to be pitied are the guilt-ridden. Like heavy smog, guilt pollutes and depresses them. It is there when they wake in the morning. It disturbs their nights that can lead to a life of sadness and end in self-destruction.

We talk glibly about sin as though we see it easily as dust or dirt. Not so. Theft we recognise. Or mugging. These foul the fairways and offend the eye. They are obvious sin. But the worst cancer is not conscious; it is concealed. Real sin suppurates in the subconscious. We cannot diagnose it. Or deal with it. Yet how it wearies and worries us. Such a sin is envy. I have never met anyone who consciously decided to be envious. Yet envy torments us all. We seek promotion and are passed over in favour of one we believe to be our inferior. Do we accept their success? We do not. We burn with resentment, we slander and our comments are acid. This is sin and we cannot release ourselves from its grip. I choose envy because I have seen too many good people let it first disfigure and finally destroy them. Yet they remain blandly unaware of the true infection; they assign their bitterness to some other cause. Adam was envious of God and burned to replace him. Goodness attracts envy far more than evil. The crowd chose Barabbas the murderer. They rejected Christ. Sin is refusal to accept Christ as the norm of the good, the true and the beautiful. It is Christ who reveals what real sin is. He sees it as separation. And he sees its first symptom as anxiety. But in an anxiety that attaches itself to no particular thing, a floating anxiety that ticks within us at work and play, in company or in solitude. Christ takes anxiety as primary evidence of rooted and original sin. Equally, the Church does not underrate the ravages of anxiety. Like Christ, it sees sin and anxiety as riding in tandem. So many sins are the sour fruit of an anxiety we cannot assuage, cannot even uncover.

Anxiety

We are anxious only because we are not at one with our origin. In God we have our origin. In him we move and have our being; not our well-being. To be is to be with God; and so with our real selves. Then we know stillness and we find strength. Nothing weakens like worry; Christ sees worry as global waste. And the source of worry is divide. The divided person gets little done; he lacks the energy. And he lacks the attention. Whatever he is doing, he feels he should be doing something else. If at play, he feels he should be working. If on holiday, he feels he should be making money instead of making merry. He is two people and each reproaches the other. This is a sad condition. And this is the raw condition of sin.

Our true origin is in God. He is our still centre. Adam envied God and sought autonomy. He broke with God and decided to be his own divinity. He manufactured a new origin, one grounded on separation from God. He, not God, would decide what was good, what was evil. He would be his own guide, his own good, his own god. No longer was his origin in his Maker. His origin would be in himself. This separation is sin and it erupts in anxiety, for no longer does he know who he is, what he is for, why he is here. Anxiety festers here. Guilt, shame and sorrow breed and multiply in the heart of man, woman and child.

The forgiving God

Yet not everyone. Jesus reveals in his person that sin is not necessary. He is sinless, not because he is God, but because he is man. True man. Sin is not the human but the sub-human. As he walks the villages of his country, Jesus reveals that God and man want each other. "I and the Father are one" is no pious metaphor but stark reality. In him there is no sin, no separation, no radical anxiety. He is, simply, man, Man he ought to be. Not a second Abraham, not a second Moses. But a second Adam. He does not disown his ancestry. For the sin of Adam is not determinative of history. Jesus reveals that sin is not the first force in the world. In Christ man recovers his origin. Original sin is not decisive. A new word has been spoken. The noun is "forgiveness".

Forgiveness is not really understood simply because it is not logical. Logic is human and logic is hard. It stands on the ethic of reprisal and retaliation. If he hurts me, I will hurt him. Hence, wars, strikes, the vendetta. It is man's classic solution to the pain of hurt. "An eye for an eye." So Jesus is speaking a new language and offending a universal code when he asserts "Do good to them that hate you". This is not the voice of sin but the sound of salvation. For I oppose God. And he does not retaliate, does not demand retribution. Every hour of every day we survive on forgiveness. A punishing god would be a monster; a violent god would make atheists of us all. To believe in Christ is to believe that I breathe the oxygen of forgiveness. Christ comes simply for the forgiveness of sins. The world does not understand forgiveness. It is new wine, the ooze of unusual grapes. It is not connivance, not the blind eye. It cannot be cased in the categories of law like a suspended sentence. Forgiveness is total restoration of a person beaten and broken by the weight of sin. Forgiveness has breadth. It is a total medicine. It deals with depression, that pervading malady which pills may palliate but not remove. It restores self-esteem to those whom failure leads to the hell of self-disgust. It gives back to man his future. It is the antidote to that brittle cynicism which is the armour of the witty who inwardly despair of God and people. Above all, it is the force that can handle fear. "Fear not, it is I" is the anthem of the forgiver.

Jesus spends his nights and days in revealing the forgiving God. It is no easy exercise. No one naturally believes in forgiveness. "You get what you pay for"; that is the secular gospel. Nothing is for free; this is the theology of the market. And it is inevitable that people will project this crude commerce on to God.

H

Hence, human sacrifice to pagan gods, hence holocausts and hecatombs and random slaughter. Hence, fear and a life of interior trepidation. This is disease. And this is the great corruption. We are at odds with the creator, his creation.

Jesus reveals we can do nothing about sin. It is too large, too lethal. "Without me you can do nothing." We cannot barter with God. But we want to. For if we can do a deal, then we are his equal and can level with him, get even with his excellence. This is sin's great ambition, first insinuated by the serpent and still seductive. The admitted sinner did not disturb Christ. For him and her he had words of tenderness. It was the upright, those stiff with moral rectitude that terrified him. For their sin was plated with gold and paraded behind a facade engaging to the eye. Yet there was nothing behind. Just evil and emptiness. They did not believe they were in need of forgiveness. And this sin disables even God. The contrite seek forgiveness. The complacent deny its need. They have no faith in God. For all faith converges on forgiveness. And forgiveness can offend our pride.

Jesus has only one sermon and its text is almost too simple: "Your sins are forgiven; your faith has made you whole." Notice that the opposite of sin is not moral excellence. It is faith. Conscious virtue can lead away from God and persuade us to believe that we have won the prize by our own practices. There were many in Christ's audience who felt no need of forgiveness. Hard people. Yet, seemingly, holy people. Tragedy occurs when holiness is at odds with humanity. Yet true holiness is truly human and Jesus is its evidence. Holiness is wholeness and displays itself as beauty. Beauty is goodness speaking to us all in language of great appeal. It is Christ who earths the divine fire on this chilly planet.

The rebellious teenager

Forgiveness has beauty. The most moving stories in the gospel impart that peace we experience in the presence of goodness and beauty. Such is the parable of the prodigal son. It has passed into the anthology of every language for it conveys the wonder of this

106

divine force we call forgiveness. Yet it is not a moral tale. Far from it. Moral tales stand on justice. They end predictably with reward for good, with retribution for evil. These are the stories that entrance children and bore adolescents. In a sense, they do not ring true. Life is not like that. Life is far more mysterious than morality. Innocence suffers. Evil succeeds. Apparently. That is the mystery.

We have all met the prodigal son, the rebellious teenager. We have all experienced that adolescent urge which finds home too restrictive, parents too puritan, and old values questionable. The young man is the son of a wealthy farmer and is tired of the plough. He seeks the lights of the secular city. The father is wise; he knows this boy. He lets him go. This boy must learn as the impetuous learn — by experience. He has money. So he has friends. The money runs out. So do the friends. An early lesson painful to all. He is reduced to near-despair. Only one saving emotion remains, some faith in his father. Not in his love. In his justice. He will return as a servant, abdicate as a son. His life will be devoted to repayment. A very moral, Sunday-school tale. Goody-goody stuff.

Then all goes wrong. We understand a parable only when it goes wrong, when it conflicts with what we think should happen. The boy has prepared a florid confession. It is never finished. For the father is unique and has appeared in no novel or drama. He treats this wastrel like royalty. Robe, ring, meal, music. How extravagant is forgiveness. How liberal is love. How fine and how foolish. Round that table with the music and wine the son is reborn, remade and finds good company. And true communion. The test is always communion. The father does not call him a servant. Or even a sinner. He calls him a son. Indeed, he remakes his son.

There is an empty chair round that table. The elder son is a key to this parable. For he has a case. He stands for morality. As with Shylock his plea is justice. He wants the prodigal punished. His argument cannot be faulted if we accept his premiss. For he has not offended and has received no reward, no supper, no celebration. The father listens and concurs. Yet he does not retract, does not apologise for his conduct. He insists that forgiveness is the only agent of restoration. True, in terms of the market and common morality forgiveness is folly. Justice looks coldly on forgiveness. Justice wants punishment; death. Forgiveness is illogical, the great loner in life. It wants to restore, to bring the diseased to health, the dead to life. "He who was dead is alive again." That is a divine deed. Only forgiveness can work this miracle. Forgiveness cannot be bought. It comes duty free.

It is easy to identify with the prodigal. Possible to identify with the father. But impossible to identify with the elder son. Yet that is the point. The sins of the just are the real impediment. The church-goer with the acid tongue. The priest obsessed with money. Hamlet sick with revenge. What is the sin of the elder son? It is hard to detect. He is loyal, industrious, pious. A good son. But not yet a brother. And the fatherhood of God speaks only in the brotherhood of man. The elder boy cannot forgive. And the test is forgiveness. No other. God bears no grudges. Nor should we.

The size of forgiveness

We must identify with those who find forgiveness too hard. Then we know ourselves. And then we catch a gleam of the gospel light. For the gospel is crazy paving; its stories do not slot into our mean and moral categories. Simon the Pharisee is outraged that Jesus should allow Magdalen to anoint him. She is a sinner. Yes, says Jesus, a sinner but forgiven; she loves much. And forgiveness is loving much, too much for mere morality. But let us not criticise Simon or the Pharisees for they are not the exceptions but the rule. They live within us all. Peter did not understand forgiveness and sought to quantify it, to make it purchase. Judas did not believe in forgiveness but in repayment. And how appalling the cost of his unfaith. The wages of this sin is death.

A forgiving God is the only bearable God. Justice lacks the wine of salvation. The justice of God is the love of God and cannot be cut to human size. Shylock is the classic figure of human justice as the only norm of common living. And in the great trial scene his case is unanswerable. There is impasse. Until Portia, the judge in disguise, speaks three lines which carry the cadence of Christianity.

> . . . therefore Jew
> Though justice be thy plea, consider this:
> That in the course of justice none of us
> Would see salvation.

We have sympathy for Shylock as his plea is so human. The resistance to Christ is the resistance of the human to the divine, of justice to love, of law to grace. Possibly, we understand forgiveness only when we experience it. Only when our hearts are broken and our life in ruins, our good name gone, and our hope hopeless. And someone comes from nowhere and by an unexpected word and an unexpected love restores us to life and futurity. We call him or her an angel. There is no other word. For the angel stands in the presence of the Holy. And the angel does God's bidding. And his command is to forgive. We can say no more.

THE RESURRECTION OF THE BODY

"There is another man inside of me, and he is angry with me." So wrote a pessimistic theologian. At times we share his pessimism and suffer from the demon of disquiet. Each of us seems to be a walking war; a civil war. Often we name the opponents and call them body and soul. It is a fatal misreading of the human constitution.

Spiritual writers can be so unhelpful. The epithets they apply to the body are often so derogatory. "A carcass." "A prison." Christian pessimism breeds in this malarial swamp and its disease is contagious. For the body is indispensable; the body is good; the body is made for glory. For body and soul are not two distinct entities destined to endless contact. Each person is one. We are not bisected, not uneasy compounds, with a noble element bonded to an ignoble. Each of us is single; an animated body, not a juxtaposition of opposed entities. The Jews held firm to this truth. The Greeks, alas, saw the body as roughage and impediment. And this dualism has scarred much Christian spirituality.

When Christ seeks to relay his real presence he says "This is my body". Body is the most eloquent word he can employ to convey the presence of his personality. His total personality. He is not referring to mere matter, but to the totality of his person. We still employ this ourselves in part. We say "he is somebody". Or, damagingly, "he is a nobody". We cannot understand Christ unless we see him as he saw himself — as one harmonious personality. True, there is conflict in us all. But the contestants and not body and soul. The war is between spirit and spirit; the whole person at odds with the whole person. What we call "sins of the flesh" are, in fact, sins of the spirit.

Resurrection and release

The resurrection of the body simply means a total resurrection. But not from the body. This would be vandalism; God is no vandal. In becoming human, in putting on flesh, he was not slumming on our behalf. He was not condescending nor acting a menial role. He was revealing the quality of humankind and pointing to its destiny. Mankind feels contained, boxed-in, and seeks space and light and liberation. Liberation from drag and drudgery from the things that make living too confined. This aspiration is universal. "Oh, for the wings of a dove" sings the psalmist. Resurrection is the oldest song and we envy the bird its power to rise, for this is a fine symbol of elevation. How we admire the lark, its pride of flight, its power to soar and survey the sky. No wonder so many nations find their emblem in the eagle. Yet the bird cannot fly without wings and its flight is limited by its wing-span. Man lives within limits. Each of us has one talent. This is personality. And the spark of personality is Spirit. Spirit is animation. It is ignition. And it is invisible. It needs a means of articulation if we are to receive its power and know its presence. Only the body gives it voice and vocabulary. God is pure spirit; no man knows him by straight vision. Christ is his word and sound and epiphany. Not a visual aid or an audio aid, but a total incarnation. Yet within the limits that flesh imposes. Christ too admired the birds of the air. And he, too, felt the press and imprisonment of confinement. The Spirit is willing. The flesh is weak and mutes its elocution. This is pain; our reach is larger than our grasp. So we sigh for release; we seek resurrection. To be our true and unfettered selves.

Resurrection and life

The child at the font is naturalised into the rhythm of resurrection. It is baptised not to save its soul, but to save itself. Its destiny is not to become an angel but another Christ, renovated, realised, risen. Resurrection is growth and Christ too had to grow in wisdom and stature. All life is growing and Jesus is not merely the life, but the life and resurrection. The two are inseparable as thirst and water. We thirst for a larger life and are pained by the dryness of daily existence. Christ offers living water, water that will fertilise our little faith. His work is resurrection. It is a total work. He has high regard for the body and does not see it as shoddy stuff, but as matter for glory. So he heals and nourishes those afflicted with disease or hunger. And, in his last donation, he imparts his life in totality, body, blood, soul, divinity. It is the risen Christ we receive in the Eucharist.

We can learn much from the saint and artist. They pass on the light of resurrection and diminish our dimness. In great art we see Spirit embodied in paint or glass or stone. Even in our agnostic world the Spirit will not be denied admiration. The cathedral presents the Spirit in place; the Sunday presents the Spirit in time. The artist who carved the finials or painted the glass was not a technician. He was more. The glory of the great cathedral is not its design or attitude. It is the Spirit it incarnates, the inspiration. There is no beauty without truth and even the agnostic is drawn to the cathedral if only because he cannot do otherwise. Here is a world removed from that of the supermarket or stock exchange. Here is height and nobility and half-remembered sanctity. Here is the impress of the holy; its towers rising to the great spaces of the sky.

All faith converges on resurrection. But how impoverished is resurrection if seen as rejecting the body which is so much our own. This makes for a bloodless spirituality short on joy and suspicious of laughter. To disown the body is to deny our creation and to see the world of things and people as dull and dismal. It is to mutilate creation. It is to dishonour the creator who sees his handiwork as good. The body is creation and is sublime. The great artist seeks to convey something of the mystery of the human form for it is the image of the divine magnificence. In the great artist, head and heart and hand conspire to explore the human body and to convey something of its mystery. And a great Madonna and Child — the prototype of all art — frees the personality from tautness and expands the outlook. Faith is reinforced and we see the human form as made for transformation. Resurrection is the revelation which believes that man has a destiny that is divine. And art is a manifestation; spirit eloquent in the common things of creation.

The saint is an artist of living and resurrection in his dream. He disciplines the body but does not deny its excellence. He is aware that the body seeks autonomy and see its needs as primary. It needs to know its place as a sanctuary of the Spirit. He fasts, not for reasons of self-destruction. Mortification is for vivification, for life, not death. The body, if overindulged, will die and have no home for the Spirit. Resurrection is of the whole personality and demands discipline and self-denial. For there is a death-instinct in us all and when the pain of things is too great we want to end it all. This is to disbelieve, to deny our destiny, and to live without hope. The question that hangs suspended over us all is stark. Will my life end in something or in nothing? Will it be ascension or decline? Will I know resurrection or slide into hell and hopelessness? In some religious systems human destiny is to be dissolved into some vast, amorphous pool where personality dissolves. It is a kind of benign extinction.

For Christians personality is realised, fully made and fully matured in resurrection. And resurrection is total, not a liberation from the body but its perfection; a completion of the person, body and soul. Jesus never speaks slightingly of the body. For him it is the symbol of personality, and resurrection of the body is resurrection of the person. Only a diseased theology will see the body as encumbrance and sometimes as evil. Then arises that deadly dualism which sees creation divided into spirit which is good and matter which is squalid. This makes life unbearable. Spirituality becomes strain; pleasure something to fear and fly from. Christianity becomes an unloved and unlovely thing. Eternally opposed to the colours and contrasts of creation, to the diversity of people, to the songs and symphonies of given things. The great sin becomes to take pleasure in life. Such a travesty of truth. The great sin is not to believe in Christ who died and was raised in his totality. There is an attractive wholeness in true Christianity and the creed gives it voice in the resurrection of the body. Of each man, each woman who believes. And believing has life, here and hereafter.

LIFE EVERLASTING

"Enjoy yourself now — you'll be a long time dead." This is the theology of the factory floor, the grim creed of many of our contemporaries. Death is extinction. Life has no point. Life is coping.

We cannot prove there is an after-life. Philosophy offers some ingenious arguments. They may persuade; they never convince. The most persuasive argument derives from a conviction that life has purpose, that good should find reward and that man is more than a chemical compound. There is in him some Spirit, a spark, which is not to die in the grave for it is stronger than death and dissolution. This conviction persists even in an uncertain century.

Chesterton once remarked that he would rather live crucified than not live at all. We can excuse the excess and still see sincerity in his remark. The Greeks would have endorsed his desire. One of their thinkers said the Greeks would prefer an after-life of torment rather than annihilation. They were a people in love with life; the great dread was extinction. The Jews had only a slender hold on an after-life. There is occasionally a lilt of hope that all flesh will see salvation, but their religion settled for Sheol, a place of lifelessness, of a kind of conscious annihilation, of existence without pain or pleasure or purpose. This shadow-life mystifies the imagination. To die was to descend into Sheol.

Christianity is bold in its belief in an after-life. Indeed, life is the vibrant noun in the New Testament and Jesus defines his mission simply — to impart life and a larger life. God is life without inhibition, and man is instinct with this desire for a life rimmed by no horizon, unclouded by fears of death or diminution, by loss or loneliness. The fullness of life means life with God for there is no life drawn from any alternate source. So, to say "I believe in God" is already to assert that "I believe in life ever-lasting".

The word "everlasting" can mislead. It suggests time going on and on. Nothing could be more unbearable, no matter how plush the surrounds or how elegant the furnishings. "Eternal" is probably a better word. It excludes the monotony of too much time. For life eternal refers not to quantity but to a heightened quality of life, an experience that lies beyond the best imagination. St John asserts that we know what we are. But we do not know what we shall be. This is a wise agnosticism. For theatrical scenarios of heaven are infantile or ludicrous. They do Christianity harm by the trivia and toys they provide as answer to man's aspirations.

All man wants is love and love cannot be depicted. He experiences love in this life but it is fire under threat of extinction. Yet it is the one experience that exalts and it takes him into a world where words are insufficient. It is more than a human experience. It is new wine and makes him do dangerous things. "Greater love than this no man has; he will lay down his life for his friends." Love has this peculiar conviction that it is stronger than death. To die for the loved one is not folly.

Heaven

The word "heaven" is one which will not go away. It is indispensable to song; it is the theme of the love-song. It occurs in conversation when we seek to describe an experience of joy beyond common satisfaction; it is an experience which breaks the rules of routine living. It is more than pleasure, more than euphoria. We rely on words like "rapture", "bliss", "ecstasy". These have no clear meaning. For the great experiences cannot be spoken. They belong to the mystic and the mystic can only stammer and exclaim. He cannot describe. Prose is too club-footed. Poetry can only suggest and evoke.

Every religious system has its heaven. The primitive picture is one of plenty, of food and wine in abundance. To people living lives of destitution one can understand this fiction. Heaven is absence of hunger. And a life of hunger is a life of hell. Perhaps we best understand heaven from our idea of hell. Great and successful generals have said "War is hell". Heaven, then, is peace and concord. But what is common to all people is that they carry within them some rough outline of heaven and hell. These are the two brackets of their existence. To transform society from hell to heaven is the great enterprise. The French of the eighteenth century found the corruption of the Bourbon regime made life hell. They sought to create heaven. The means — revolution. The guillotine was the blade of salvation. And an English poet wrote a memorable couplet:

> Bliss was it in that dawn to be alive
> And to be young was very heaven.

Alas, heaven fell short of expectation. There was blood and war and tyranny. A better hell but no heaven. Yet the dream persists and the revolutionary is the dreamer. He attracts by a promise. A promise of heaven on earth, of peace and plenty, of a society without class or conflict, where all are equal and there is no avarice.

Jesus believes in heaven. He does not see it in a change of structure, in political adjustment, in economic reform. These are superficial and will not answer the real need. The true change is radical; too radical for the radicals. It is a change of heart. And a change so deep that man is incapable of achieving it by resolution. So people do not understand him. There were zealots and revolutionaries among his following and these wanted to make him king. For everyone talked of the kingdom. But the talk was at cross-purposes. For the human idea of kingship was not Christ's. They saw him as a Jewish Caesar who would lead them into battle, win the fight and leave them the field. For Jesus this was human thinking and the human way. It would bring carnage. It would not bring the kingdom.

For Jesus the kingdom has its seat in the human heart. Each heart is a divided heart. And world conflict is the conflict of the heart amplified into class against class, and nation against nation. Begin with the heart for there the kingdom has its home. But is

117

there one whose heart is whole and holy? There is one. He can say "I am the life" and that life is not to be hoarded but to be given, and recklessly. The death of Christ is the real revelation. He is the authentic leader. The true leader dies for his people. He is the victim. The kingdom is born of a dying. The victim precedes the victor. This does not square with human thinking. Christ disowns kingship as understood by us all. The true kingdom needs no court or courtiers, no police, no army. It needs heart.

This is hard to understand and only the resurrection of Christ discloses the scale of his revolution. In human terms his death is failure and the kingdom still-born. But the kingdom took fire and remains with us, imperfect, half-realised, but there. Those who acknowledge Christ as Son and Saviour already have one foot in the kingdom. They experience the life and proclaim the values which Christ revealed as eternal. In the eyes of the world they may seem foolish. Foolish to renounce wealth, power, marriage, prestige. St Paul coined the phrase "Fools for Christ's sake". No man was more aware of the wrenching character of lived Christianity. He himself had undergone a change of heart so violent that he was a new man. He had always been deeply religious and the most fanatical of Jews. Now he saw the kingdom and it was not Jewish or Gentile, male or female, slave or free. It was universal, and was not a human edifice. Its stone was Christ and he alone gives it firmness and foundation.

"To live", said Paul, "is Christ". And then the rider, "to die is gain". This dying begins with baptism and to be christened is to find a new centre of gravity. The "ego" is the enemy. It wants to be first. But the first will be the last in the kingdom. This is the meaning of humility for humility is "humus", good soil where tall trees grow. And humility is not natural to man. And all humility is before God. It sees life as coming only from him. And the grammar of humility is the life — and death — of Christ. Humility is realism. It sees the world as God's world and true life as a given thing. Because we are born in sin and separation from God we cannot find the life on our own. But we try to. There lies our pride. Sin is refusal to see in Christ the way made clear, the truth disclosed, the life imparted. Humility is a receiving heart and so many hearts are glazed and unreceptive.

118

Life everlasting begins on this earth. There can be no after-life if there is no before-life. Those who do not know God cannot desire to live with him. Heaven or hell is our option. God sends no one to hell. Hell, like heaven, is chosen and we make the choice here not hereafter. God respects choice and we have the power to prefer to go it alone and devise a heaven of our own fabrication. Yet God is not mocked. The world which seeks to build Jerusalem of man-made materials will find it has created just another hell. This century has known many revolutions. Too many. Yet the kingdom is too often composed of camps and commissars. The new regimes are more brutal than those they deposed.

The Requiem Mass is a most moving celebration and its chant is of everlasting life. It ponders with great beauty two themes — light and rest. It is aware that much of the pain of living consists in darkness, in that inability to understand ourselves and our experience. So much suffering seems wanton and wasteful. Faith falters and life grows pale. We need a greater light, one that will not die with the dark; an eternal and unoccluded light. We need a vision denied us in this life. An intimacy with God and people, a realisation of the point of things. This is a quality of life we may glimpse here below but fitfully, in sudden flashes that die as soon as born. In heaven we shall see God not through smoked glasses but as he is, luminous as love.

The second theme of the Requiem Mass is rest. Perhaps "re-quies" is better translated as "refreshment". For rest can suggest inertia and who could abide a static heaven? In heaven there will be activity but without strain, action without fatigue, worship without weariness. So we pray that the loved one now deceased will enter that kingdom only half-realised on earth and now live the life without the pain that secular life imposes. "Eternal rest grant unto them, O Lord." "And let perpetual light shine upon them." Light and rest we seek here below and never find them in their fullness. Yet we know them in prayer and liturgy if too briefly.

Teachers and preachers often present heaven as a place. This is all very well if that place is home. And home is more than a house. Home is not where we live; home is where we are loved.

People have a homing instinct and the desire for home is a universal desire. For at home there is company and fire and freedom. Hell is loneliness, absolute and unabated. Heaven is being and belonging. "Hell", said a philosopher, "is other people." Clearly the utterance of an unhappy heart. For if we seek to impale heaven in one noun it must be a hackneyed one. It must be "relationship". To live is to relate, and every relationship involves hurt as well as happiness. Except one. God is relationship without discord, love without stress. Heaven is the home where there will be freedom from death and disappointment. We shall see God as he is. He will receive us as sons and daughters. And with him we shall shed all loneliness and find love that satisfies. Totally and eternally.